Taking the Harder Right

Taking the Harder Right

By Oliver G. Halle

Contributing Authors
Diann Cattani
Josh Kenyon
Walt Pavlo

Concord Bridge Press
Smyrna, Georgia

©2006 Oliver G. Halle. All rights reserved. Printed in the United States of America on acid-free paper. No part of this publication may be reproduced or distributed in any form or by any means or stored in a database or retrieval system without the prior written permission of the publisher.

www.CorporateScaredStraight.com

FIRST EDITION   2 3 4 5 6 7 8 9
First printing, March 2006
Second printing, April 2007

ISBN 0-9772830-0-3

Published by   Concord Bridge Press
                    www.ConcordBridgePress.com
                    4029 Benell CT
                    Smyrna GA 30082

Editors: Edward M. Buckner (ed@buckners.us) and Lois B. Buckner

Book & Cover Design: Kim Wayman (art) & Edward M. Buckner

Back Cover Photograph: Oliver G. Halle

> Make us to choose the harder right instead of the easier wrong, and never to be content with a half truth when the whole truth can be won.
>
> —from the Cadet Prayer,
> United States Military Academy,
> West Point

Oliver G. Halle

Dedication

This book is dedicated to my father and mother, **Knut and Ruth Halle**. *They laid the foundation for living a moral and ethical life, not by words but by their example.*

Oliver G. Halle

Acknowledgements

In writing a book such as this there were many influences and influential people that helped to form the fabric of the content. Well over thirty years ago, I was a twenty-one-year-old ensign on board my first ship, the USS SPRINGFIELD (a light cruiser with a complement of 1,500) where I served under executive officer Commander Warren C. Hamm. Commander Hamm went on to retire as a rear admiral. It was his rigid enforcement of the rules mixed with quiet compassion that taught me the importance of having a firm set of standards. The commanding officer of the ship, Captain Lando Zech, was a leader whose command presence was manifested by a military bearing that was firm but never loud. He retired as a vice admiral. Their two leadership styles, while different, were complementary and for a young impressionable man, they contributed to the moral and ethical fabric and the person I became.

In my long career with the FBI as a special agent I had the fortune of working with many other agents and federal prosecutors. I was proud to be associated with these people, too numerous to name, who demonstrated the utmost integrity. They faced difficult moral and ethical decisions every day and genuinely tried to take the harder right instead of the easier wrong when faced with making them. Their high standards of honesty and integrity served the public well and over the years added to the fabric.

The cover of this book was designed by Kim Wayman. Kim is an amateur artist and student at Brown University. In my opinion her drawing captures the essence of ***Taking the Harder Right***. She understood the theme and was able to translate it into a work of art. I wish to acknowledge Kim's contribution and talent and thank her for her work.

My three teenage children, Caitlyn, Victoria, and Tyler, continue to be important threads to the moral and ethical fabric. They are a constant reminder to me of the importance of setting the example and paying forward what I can't pay back to my predecessors. I am grateful to my wife, Mollie, for encouraging me to share my experiences and for the support she provided.

I owe a debt of gratitude to Josh Kenyon, Diann Cattani, and Walt Pavlo for their chapters in this book. They opened their hearts and bared their souls in sharing the experiences that devastated their lives. Each struggled to regain a measure of their former life, and they chose to do this in the hope that others will learn from them. They deserve a second chance, and I hope for them that perhaps there will be readers who will give it to them.

Lastly, I want to extend a special thanks to Ed and Diane Buckner. The Buckners were the editors of this book, but they were also much more. After attending one of the seminars they were emphatic that this book needed to be written. Writing those first few words is always the most difficult part, and Ed and Diane gently prodded and nudged until I got started. Their patience at times was above and beyond what anyone could rightfully expect. Without their help this book would not have been written.

—Oliver G. Halle
January 2006

Editors' Note
Ed and Diane Buckner

We've known and loved Oliver Halle for many years, enjoying his company socially, bragging to other friends that we knew an FBI agent, and introducing houseguests to Halle. Everyone who has met him has agreed with us that Halle is a good storyteller as well as our good friend. When he told us about the seminar on practical ethics he'd put together, it sounded interesting, like everything else he's done. For a year or two, we heard occasional reports from him about the presentations, though we didn't realize just how many of them he was doing. In fall 2004 he invited us to come hear the program at a local university, and we gladly accepted. Because we knew Oliver Halle and a bit about the seminar, we had pretty high hopes for the evening.

Our expectations were far short of the mark. Halle and two of his associates we'd never met—Josh Kenyon and Diann Cattani—spoke to a class of perhaps fifty graduate business students. Most if not all of these students were probably working full time, many of them as responsible managers already. They were old enough to be jaded and no doubt tired enough from already putting in a full day at work to sit on automatic pilot through a presentation if the speeches were dull. For over two hours the three presenters held the students—and us—spellbound. All three, it turns out, are good storytellers, and the story they told was gripping. We happened to be off to one side of the class, in desks facing the students as well as the speakers, so we were able to observe everyone in the room. We heard laughter and impassioned questions, we saw tears in people's eyes, we saw what seemed to be signs of anxiety or even fear, we saw many signs of intense interest, and we saw people literally on the edge of their seats. What we didn't see or experience ourselves were minds wandering. We heard an inspiring, powerful, important message, one dramatically and effectively hammered home.

At a recent family gathering, someone asked us why this seminar (and this book that has grown out of the seminar) was important, why it was even needed. After all, "Don't people really know what's right, whether they do it or not? Really, what's the point?" Oliver Halle always tells seminar participants, near the start of the workshop, that the program is not for career criminals, not for determined cheaters or thieves. "In fact," he always says, "if that's you, we'll be wasting your time and you can save us all a lot of trouble if you want to leave now." No one ever has, of course. But if it's not for criminals, who is it for? Halle and associates are not there, in the seminars or in this book, to teach people right from wrong or to analyze carefully the philosophical underpinnings of a sound ethical system. They don't delve into the subtle moral questions that society wages culture wars to resolve. They're not there to nag any of us, to harangue us about our integrity, or to threaten us. They assume that their listeners or readers have some ethical standards in common, that we all value honesty, decency, families, and the respect of our peers.

Halle and company are not really even, except as an indirect byproduct of their message, trying to save companies or other organizations money or to protect organizational reputations. The purpose is straightforward and easily understood: it is to make clear, in ways these presenters are astonishingly well equipped to communicate, the terrible things that can happen to people who have a good, sound code of ethics, who have been raised and educated well, who know right from wrong, and who care. People, probably like you, who have much to lose— self-respect, reputations, jobs, and even families. The purpose is also to show how easy it is to slip, even for good people with good foundations of morality. And how insidiously one small slip can lead to another. It is at times an emotional case they make, but it is well grounded, thoughtful, and rationally strong; and it is never dull.

A crucial part of the purpose of the program and the book is to make explicit the important, practical connection between leadership and ethics. This program says and shows that strong effective ethics in an organization depend on good leaders. Halle has shared with us over the years the influence of some of the leaders that helped to shape his life as a young naval officer, and two of these leaders went on to become prominent Navy Admirals.

Those business students that night in fall 2004 aren't the only ones subject to being a little jaded. The two of us have heard, between us, hundreds of in-service presentations, continuing education classes, and lectures of all kinds. Some of these have been good, but too many have been dull and dry even when they conveyed important information. And some of the ones we've heard that were not dull or dry, the ones often given by big name presenters, were more effective as entertainment than as education—lines that made us feel good or laugh instead of lessons that made us think, that changed our behavior or attitudes. Jokes, sometimes worth retelling, rather than memorable, telling points. After we heard Halle and associates, we found ourselves still talking about what they said days later, and we kept telling each other that we wished many thousands of people could hear them, not just a few students and us. Finally, we talked Halle into letting us be involved, doing some of the behind-the-scenes work, promoting the seminars, and editing this book. We're proud to be connected to ***Taking the Harder Right***. We hope that you have extraordinarily high expectations as you read; you won't be disappointed.

Oliver G. Halle

Table of Contents

1. Introduction 1
2. **Ethical Principles** 7
3. **How Good People Get Into Trouble** 15
4. **Truth is Stranger Than Fiction: The Story of Romeo Mike, Part I** 29
5. **Character Matters: Fear of Punishment and Hope of Reward** 35
6. **Life-Changing Versus Life-Shaping Experiences** 39
7. **Going Back to One's Code** 45
8. **The Story of Romeo Mike, Part II** 49
9. **The Courage to Live** 71
10. **From Ambitious and Upwardly Mobile to Miserable and Broke in Under a Decade** 91
11. **Conclusion** 111

Oliver G. Halle (Note on the Author) 113

Index 115

1 Introduction

Good people get into trouble. Good people are those who know right from wrong, who have a moral and ethical compass, and who honestly try to live lives that comport with these values. This book is about these people. It is about you, your next-door neighbor, the civic club member, the person you fellowship with, your office cubicle mate, or your best friend. Understanding how this can happen to anyone is difficult, but it is important to state at the outset that this book is not intended for someone with a criminal mind. Someone bent on stealing, committing fraud, or otherwise engaging in unethical, immoral, and illegal behavior will not be deterred by this book. This story is intended to sensitize good people to the pitfalls of life that they never imagined could happen to them. It is also worth noting that this is not intended to be a philosophical or psychological treatise on the subject; it is a practical analysis of the problem, one designed to help good people learn the risks and avoid them.

I spent twenty-eight years as a special agent with the Federal Bureau of Investigation (FBI), and the last seventeen years were devoted to the investigation of corrupt public officials, a particular variety of white collar crime. As the years went by I noticed that many of the people who were getting into trouble and coming under the microscope of the FBI were good people. The question came up over and over: how could this happen? Is there a way to deter people from getting caught up in similar situations? In the fall of 1999, a precipitating event occurred that convinced me that I should share my experience with a wider audience in the hope that some good could come out of my experiences and particular vantage point. I talk about this event in a separate chapter, called "The Story of Romeo Mike, Part I." It is a story that lives up to the old adage that sometimes truth can be stranger than fiction.

The writer Willa Cather said that "there are only two or three human stories in this world, and they go on repeating themselves as ferociously as though they never happened before" (*O Pioneers!*, 1913). There are so many problems that people deal with each day, and so many of these people do not understand that their problems are not unique. They range from financial difficulties, health, divorce, family abuses, bad bosses at work, unfulfilling careers, ailing parents, problem children, and on and on. Anyone reading this almost certainly can identify with one or more of these situations. It is in time of such stresses that one's judgment can become clouded, leading to bad choices and decisions. Too often the wrong choices will result in a lifetime of bad consequences. There is no one solution to prevent someone who thinks his life is out of control from exercising poor judgment. In this world we are all connected, and reaching out for help through a variety of sources is one way to realize that your problem is not unique. "The mass of men lead lives of quiet desperation," said Henry David Thoreau (*Walden*, 1854). But we do know that you are not alone, and that is the first step to understanding that there are alternatives to deal with life's burdens.

Some years ago when I was assigned to the New York Office of the FBI, I had an experience that got my attention and which has stayed with me. The Securities and Exchange Commission (SEC) had identified some very unusual trading. The purchasers of certain shares were all middle- to lower-income people who had never owned stock before. Suddenly they were spending thousands of dollars to buy stock in companies that were about to be merged, acquired, or taken over. The SEC identified a very prominent law firm as the common denominator for all of these transactions. Such transactions are handled with the utmost secrecy because of the impact rumors can generate that can influence the value of the stock in the respective companies. One of the traders was an organized crime figure who owned a jewelry store and who had no plausible way to know anything about the subject companies. Trading on inside information is a felony, and the SEC turned over the criminal investigation of this matter to the FBI.

With an SEC attorney I met with the managing partner of the firm to discuss the situation and to try to identify the insider. Months went by with every suspect being washed out because of insufficient evidence or a verifiable alibi. There were about thirty people in the firm who conceivably had access to the relevant information, but narrowing down this group to one or two suspects was the problem. Ultimately the FBI approved polygraphing all of these suspects in perhaps the largest effort ever undertaken at the time. The SEC lawyer and I met with the managing partner to discuss this strategy. Up to this point he had been cooperative but only reluctantly. He could not fathom that someone in the firm could be so dishonest, and he always tried to explain away any evidence that could implicate an employee or lawyer. The polygraph suggestion really raised his hackles. He argued that his firm hired only good, honest people and that they had all been screened. Eventually he was persuaded that without the testing suspicion would remain with the firm and would only prolong the investigation.

The FBI sent a team of polygraphers from east of the Mississippi to New York, and suspect employees were scheduled for tests. All consented to it. One aspect of the polygraph is to identify the individual's reaction to a question where the subject is known to be lying. This is called a test question, and it helps the polygrapher to interpret his charts when the real question is asked. In this case that question was whether the subject traded on inside information or knew who did. During the day that the tests were performed I waited in a room both for the results and in case a polygrapher had a question. What happened next was astounding. Each subject was told in advance that the results of the test questions would not be revealed to the law firm. Only proof of complicity in the inside trading would be disclosed if there was sufficient corroboration. The test questions asked the subjects about theft related issues. The polygraph identified substantial theft in the firm. Employees admitted to stealing money from various cash funds. The firm remained open all night, and some employees confessed to taking office furniture and office supplies in quantities that they could then sell themselves. The thefts occurred systematically and over a period of years and were not one-time occurrences.

I do not know the personal circumstances of these individuals. I do know that the managing partner, before the polygraph testing, recounted a narrative on each one. Most were long-time members or employees with the firm who ostensibly had every reason to be trusted. They were all well paid and highly respected. Most were homeowners and had families. None would have displayed the least evidence that he or she was anything but a loyal employee. Had any one of these employees been caught it would have had dire consequences because the perpetrator(s) would have destroyed any hope of finding work in another firm, and very possibly the victim firm might have chosen to prosecute if the evidence was sufficient. The betrayal that these people committed was outrageous, and it opened my eyes to the scale of deceit and dishonesty seemingly good people could stoop to. As an aside, none of these employees was identified as the inside trader. Investigation later revealed it to be a ten-year office manager, well liked, trusted in the extreme, who sold the information. He ended up with a prison sentence.

By the time I retired from the FBI in August 2003, I had conceived of a program to train business groups, professional organizations, universities, and other entities in ethics, fraud prevention, and anticorruption. All three concepts neatly fit together. I wanted to put together a seminar that would do more than meet the minimal requirements of mandated ethics training that different professional associations are required to have, either by law or because their association finds it useful. It was imperative to have a program that would not only meet those requirements but also have real value and meaning long after the participants went back to their jobs and homes. The other ingredient that I knew was essential for this to work was to have a program with audience identification. Unless the audience could identify with the presenters it would be unsuccessful.

In this book you will meet three people who were highly educated, respected in their communities, very successful in their professions, and who had families—and who lost it all. All lost portions of their lives in federal prison. Their stories are compelling, riveting, and memorable. Diann came from an affluent family and had an athletic scholarship to Brigham Young University, where she majored in psychology and business. She was very successful in her employment in the small business sector. She is the mother of three young children and divorced. Josh had a triple major at Southern Methodist University and went on to earn a law degree at Pepperdine University. He was prominent enough in local government that he could get a telephone call returned from the governor. He, too, was married and has young twin daughters. Walt is a college graduate with an MBA degree from Mercer University. He had an upper management position in a major corporation. He has two children, and his marriage, as with the other two, did not survive the events that overtook him. These three people are contrite and remorseful, and they continue to pay the price of their crimes. They share their stories in the hope that others will not walk in their shoes.

The name of our seminar, **Taking the Harder Right**, comes from the cadet prayer at the United States Military Academy at

West Point, which says in part "Make us to choose the harder right instead of the easier wrong, and never to be content with a half truth when the whole truth can be won." I do not want to suggest that taking the harder right is easy. In fact, I want to be clear, and this will be illustrated throughout the book, that taking the harder right can be exceedingly hard with very painful consequences. However, taking the easier wrong all too often is a temporary solution with permanent consequences. Taking the easier wrong can be like eating a candy bar to assuage your immediate hunger only to leave you even hungrier later. It is empty calories. Taking the harder right is the theme of our program and this book. It is about you and me. I hope that the reader will not only find it useful in reaching a greater understanding of human behavior but an interesting read as the issues unfold.

2 Ethical Principles

Ethics covers a wide range of topics. Different professions have ethical rules that govern the conduct of an individual profession. For example, the ethical issues facing doctors are different in many ways from those facing lawyers. Lawyers must be keenly sensitive to conflicts of interests, and all law firms, particularly the larger ones, have trigger mechanisms in place to alert them to conflicts. On the other hand, doctors face quandaries such as what to tell a patient in certain circumstances. Is full disclosure always the best thing? Perhaps, but perhaps there are other intervening or superseding issues that can change the decision. Ethics also come into play in circumstances that have nothing to do with one's profession. Just day-to-day interaction with our families, friends, and co-workers causes us to make evaluations that affect these relationships, and in these instances there usually is no one right answer.

Life can be very pleasant and unimpeded when there are no challenges. It is when challenged that relationships can change. If the challenge is big enough, your entire life can change. The critical choices that you have to make during such times can dramatically alter the rest of your life. It is at these times that you must have an ethical foundation to survive. Ethics in some ways is like the foundation of a building. If the underpinnings are strong, the building will withstand the worst of storms. Perhaps it will be damaged, but it will still be standing. Without that foundation a building can be likened to a beautiful vacation home on a beach. When the storm hits, there is a good chance that it will not be there afterwards. An ethical foundation is no different, because there will be storms in our lives, and it will be those ethical underpinnings that will hold us together if the moorings are tight.

Ethics is part of the glue that holds us together. It is part of the social contract in which we live our lives to the fullest enjoyment, but with the understanding that we shouldn't live our lives at the expense of others. This sounds simple enough until competing interests of arguably equal merit clash. All too often there is no good resolution, only an outcome that can leave two or more parties less than satisfied. But at the end of the day, when the lights go out, you will have to know that your choice was the most honest and fair that you could make under the circumstances. Does doing the right thing come naturally? Some things should, such as not stealing, cheating on an exam, or taking the extra change at the store that is mistakenly given to you. But there are too many other situations where the answers are not obvious. The scientist Ernst Mayr said, "Genuine ethics is the result of the thought of cultural leaders. We are not born with a feeling of altruism toward outsiders, but acquire it through cultural learning. It requires the redirecting of our inborn altruistic tendencies toward a new target: outsiders" (*What Evolution Is*, p. 259).

I mentioned that it should be obvious that stealing is wrong. The Ten Commandments are very plain about this for those who look to them for guidance. There are times, though, when two moral or ethical imperatives clash. Take the hypothetical case of a family living in a home with no heat in the middle of winter. They have no money and cannot pay for fuel. Next door lives a fabulously wealthy man with enough firewood in his yard to last the next hundred winters. When asked for some firewood to keep the family and children warm, the wealthy man says no. Would it be wrong to take the firewood anyway, knowing that this person will never miss it? Without the wood the family risks sickness, misery, and possibly freezing. Even if you acknowledge that taking the firewood under the circumstances is stealing, is it justified? If not, could a case be presented when it would be justified? Are there other alternatives? I raise this simple problem only to illustrate that ethical quandaries come in many sizes and shapes.

This book is not intended to be overly philosophical. Nevertheless, studying ethics is not a precise science and it requires thought and reflection. For example, someone could be faced with a dilemma and look to advice from a religious text such as the Bible, but this could conflict with one's oath as a public official to uphold the law and the Constitution. An easy illustration comes to mind. Or is it so easy? Imagine that you are a citizen of Germany in 1938. Laws have been passed that make it illegal to employ Jews or to rent to them. Lawbreakers can be severely punished. Yours is a Christian family and you decide that you will allow a Jewish family to rent an apartment from you, but this family will be given false Christian documents. The police come to you one day and ask if you are renting to Jews. At that moment a myriad of thoughts go through your mind. You know that if you turn the Jewish family in, there will be dire consequences for them. You also know that if you are caught lying, you and your family will face dire consequences. You also know what is ultimately right. Is there a right answer to this? Many would say yes but with a qualifying "but." Others would respond that even if it is an unjust law, good members of a society have a duty to obey it to maintain order. The issue then becomes, what is an unjust law? And are there degrees of injustice that require different answers?

Another example of a moral and ethical conflict arose during the 2004 U.S. Presidential campaign. Senator John Kerry was banned from taking communion by a cardinal in his church because Kerry said he would abide by the law on the issue of abortion. That stance conflicted with Catholic doctrine that does not permit abortion. There are arguments on both sides of this. I believe that if one chooses to follow any legal, moral, or ethical code in conflict with the law, following the law must prevail for a public office holder. A moral obligation may exist to try to change the law to comport with one's moral code, but this should be done through the legislative process rather than by virtue of holding public office.

The Greek writer of tragic drama Sophocles said, "Rather fail with honor than succeed with fraud" (*Philoctetes*, circa 409 BCE). This is a noble principle, but when you are faced with unbearable stresses and pressures (the subject of the next chapter), can your judgment become so clouded that taking the easier wrong (fraud) overwhelms taking the harder right? Police work requires that investigators have informants. Informants are absolutely essential to making successful cases, identifying perpetrators, and preventing crimes. Developing sources is so important that when I was an FBI agent it was one of the critical elements we were graded on during our annual performance appraisal. Some years ago I met an agent at training in-service. We got to talking about our careers, past office assignments, who we mutually knew, and other things that we might have in common. It turned out we had both worked organized crime in New York, but he had preceded me by a few years. The agent narrated the following story, which points out how one's judgment can be affected because of competing interests.

The agent had arrested the son of a mob boss and charged him with some sort of theft crime involving interstate commerce. The agent approached the father and said that if the father were to help him with some investigative matters, he would guarantee that his son would get a probationary sentence. The father agreed. This had to have been a huge feather in the agent's cap. Ultimately the son pled guilty. On the day that he was sentenced the judge gave him upwards of seven years imprisonment. The agent had done absolutely nothing to meliorate the sentence. He had deceived the father in order to have a very good informant. The agent said that the father never spoke a word to him, just stared at him as everyone left the courtroom.

Were there consequences to the agent's actions? Almost certainly, but not the type you can easily measure. The agent admitted that he was embarrassed and ashamed at what he had done. On a larger scale it is a sure bet that the father, in his own way, put the word out on the street that no one should ever trust a law enforcement officer. This in turn would make it much more difficult for other investigators to develop good sources for years to come. In the short run the agent was personally successful and probably was recognized for his success. But considering the long-term consequences, would it have been better to fail with honor than to succeed with fraud? Was it more important to perhaps bring to conclusion some unsolved crimes, possibly prevent some crimes, or to have taken a different approach with the father that might not have succeeded in developing him as a source?

Larry was the vice president of a municipal enterprise. He never sought a bribe and no one ever approached him with an improper payment. One day Larry had to go out of town for a funeral. A vendor who Larry knew well happened to be in Larry's office that day. The vendor insisted that Larry take a few hundred dollars to tide him over during this unexpected emergency. Larry agreed only after it was understood that he would reimburse the vendor when he returned. But when he tried to repay the "generosity" the vendor laughed it off as an inconsequential amount of money that he was happy to provide to help a "friend" in need. Unfortunately this was the beginning of many more subtle payments that led to Larry's prosecution. What is interesting about this story, though, is that most of the money that Larry took was given to his local church. The church was new and needed funding for an organ, pews, and other costly items.

Larry had been a pillar of the community in every way. No one had a bad word to say about him. His largess with the church was recognized and only added to his stature as a selfless man, something he truly was except for this tainted money. One of the ethical considerations that arises is whether the church should return this money. You might ask who should get the money if you agree that the church should not keep it. Most would agree that Larry and the vendor should not. What about the municipality that may have paid more for the vendor's products because of the payments to Larry? Should the church keep the money arguably because it is a charitable organization? Should it be donated to a different charity? This exercise is just another illustration of the many competing interests and dilemmas that can arise to challenge your morals and ethics. There probably is no right answer, but thinking about ethical situations can help to prepare for others that lie ahead in your life.

Lawrence Rees, on p. 204 in his recent book *Auschwitz: A New History* (2005), quoted Toivi Blatt, a Holocaust survivor, as saying:

> People change under some conditions....I am only sure of one thing—nobody knows themselves....All of us could be good or bad people in [different] situations. Sometimes when somebody is really nice to me I find myself thinking, "How will he be in Sobibor?"[a Nazi death camp in Poland].

Rees noted following this quote that

> ...human beings resemble elements that are changeable according to temperature. Just as water only exists in a certain temperature range and is steam or ice in others, so human beings can become different people according to extremes of circumstances.

What any of us would do in extreme circumstances is impossible to predict, but applying ethical principles may well be more important exactly when it is hardest to predict. You will have to wrestle with these questions, and in any group you can be sure there will be different responses.

As the rest of this book will make clear, applying ethical principles is often not easy. Conscious consideration, in advance, of how you will apply them will help. But one thing is clear: you have to have strong ethical principles, or you and everyone around you may pay a terrible price. We will return to this topic in Chapter 7, "Going Back to One's Code."

3 How Good People Get Into Trouble

There are days in our lives when we wake up and declare to the world, "Isn't life great?" And it can be. There are people who seem to be problem free. They are financially comfortable; their health is good; their marriages are strong and enjoyable; the children are intelligent, well adjusted, and a true blessing; they have a strong social network, are prominent in the community, and are successful at work. Things could not really get any better. In reality, such people either do not exist or we cannot really know all that is going on in their lives. When things go badly wrong we may be challenged with difficult choices. This chapter will cover some of the things that can go wrong and how taking the harder right instead of the easier wrong may be the hardest thing you will ever have to decide to do.

Good people, who know right from wrong, can get into trouble. This can happen to people who live their lives trying to do what is right and who truly have a moral and ethical compass that points to true north. There are everyday occasions where there will be minor deviations, but good people know this and know how to correct it. None of us is perfect. Imagine that you are one of those fortunate people who has had a very good life. You recently graduated from college and are enthusiastic about entering the business world and making a positive difference. Perhaps you start your own business because you have a service that is in demand even if it is competitive. Right now the only work is government contracts. You submit a bid in response to a request for proposal for a big job. You have every expectation of getting it, and in fact you really need this contract because things have been slow lately. Much to your horror you are approached one day by a government official (let's call him "Joe") who gently explains that you have no chance of getting this contract unless you pay a kickback. Joe says that everyone in your industry "pays to play." Suddenly you realize why you have not gotten other contracts in the past.

There are a number of issues that surface with this problem. One, you have a payroll and overhead to meet. Your business is one that you cannot conduct in the private sector. Perhaps you sell a particular product such as water and wastewater equipment to municipalities, a limited market. Since everyone in this business is paying bribes, can you survive if you are the only one who does not? If you go to the authorities, will they be able to prove your allegations? Are the authorities competent to handle allegations of this type? If you cooperate with the law enforcement authorities and it is found out, will you be blacklisted from future participation in contracts? If you go out of business because you choose not to engage in doing "what everyone else is doing," will you be able to find another job? (In a small town where everyone knows everyone you could be ostracized economically and socially.) What about the mortgage on your home, the car payments, the college tuition bills that are rolling in, and the endless other financial obligations you have? Perhaps your spouse does not work, so there is no second income.

All of these issues are searing your thought processes. You wake up at night in cold sweats as you weigh off what you know to be right against all of the financial consequences that will ensue if you decide not to pay a bribe. On the other hand, you consider that since all of your competitors are paying bribes and thriving, it must be okay in some sort of sense. If you choose to pay the freight, not only will there be no adverse consequences, you will also have a very handsome payday. And besides, you deserve the contract because you do good work, and no one will get hurt because you sell a quality product. These rationalizations play on your mind.

If you choose the harder right you may very well end up unemployed or possibly bankrupt. The financial pressure will also stress you, your family, and your marriage. You will look back and ask yourself more than once if declining to pay the bribe was the sensible thing in the long run. When you see your competitor drive his BMW into the country club because he got the contract that you should have, you will be angry. Lots of emotions will run through your mind. You will be conflicted as never before in your life as you struggle each day to get back on your feet. Was it worth it?

I wish I could say that there is always a happy ending to these stories, or that justice always prevails. Unfortunately that is not true. But justice does have a way of happening more often than we might realize. In our example the struggling businessman may get a call one day from someone in law enforcement to ask about what he knows concerning kickbacks. He can recite from personal experience the attempt made on him to pay a bribe. Other testimony and evidence may lead to the prosecution of business people and government officials. What a glorious day that would be for our honest businessman who took the harder right. Or perhaps our businessman chose to take his business in a different direction and has recovered from his losses. What we do know for sure is that by living up to an ethical standard our businessman will never have to worry about the loss of his reputation, being forced out of business by the government for misconduct, or becoming a convicted felon.

Other examples of taking the harder right come to mind from my experience, although some of these examples are composites. Take the case of the young man who goes to a good law school. He has a proud academic record and is hired by a prestigious law firm. In seven to eight years he can hope to make partner. His salary grows each year, and he is making more money than he ever dreamed of. A couple of years go by and a young lady joins the firm with a similar academic pedigree. As things work out they fall in love and get married. They decide to have a family, and as is traditional in American families, they agree that she will stay home to raise the children. His income is more than ample for them to live a comfortable life and pay the typical bills of a young couple. He will be considered for partnership in another year or two. Life couldn't get any better.

One day the young lawyer's mentoring partner calls him in for a performance review. He tells the young man that the firm is pleased with his work and the 1,800 hours he billed last year, an impressive figure. However, the partner says that the firm wants him to increase his billable hours to 2,300 hours. Many people may not comprehend this number, but the best way to put it into perspective is to say that working that many billable hours does not leave much time for restroom breaks. The young lawyer hears this and quietly sighs, thinking of how hard he is already working, the subtle complaints from his wife that he is not spending enough time at home with her and the children, and how tired he is. But he agrees that he will make every effort to comply with the request. This is a good example of a boss coming into a comfortable life and turning it upside down. Just one bad boss can do that, either with unreasonable demands or by setting the tone for immoral or unethical conduct. Sometimes it's a combination of both, and there is no deadlier combination in the work place to undermine your ethics.

Six months go by. The mentoring partner calls the young attorney in for another review. The partner reminds him about their last conversation and the 2,300 hours that he was expected to bill. The partner says that he has seen no increase at all since their discussion and then adds that he does not expect to have this conversation again. The partner continues that there are plenty of young aspiring lawyers who would like to have his position in the firm. Our lawyer quickly sizes up the situation and has a panic attack. He thinks about his being the only income in their household, and while he can pay all of the bills, if he is out of work there will be no money coming in at all. He also thinks about the simple fact that the job market is such that finding another one at his current level of pay would be almost impossible, and just finding any job will be difficult. He and his wife have lived within their means, but their means have been higher than that enjoyed by most other young lawyers. This could be a recipe for disaster.

The young lawyer is frightened because he knows that billing 2,300 hours will be all but out of his reach. He is determined to try, though, but his efforts fall flat through no fault of his own. His next appraisal is coming up. He is now faced with taking the harder right or the easier wrong. The harder right will be brutally hard. He will probably lose his job. He and his wife may have to sell their home and other possessions and scale down their lifestyle. The plans they had for themselves and their children may be put off or lost forever. On the other hand, if he adds hours here and there to some of his current client's accounts, he can get his numbers up. Who would ever know, and since these are corporate clients they can well afford it. The young lawyer also thinks about the little bits of time that he may not have billed in the past. Rationalization sets in. The mentoring partner congratulates him on his hard work. All is well once again.

At one of the businesses the young lawyer serves, a sharp accountant figures out that there is no way the hours were worked that were billed to them. The company objects and threatens to take its legal business elsewhere. Our lawyer is called in for an explanation. He admits what he did when faced with incontrovertible evidence but tries to explain that the pressure consumed him to meet the firm's greater expectations.

The mentoring partner says with a straight face that he is shocked at the young man's conduct. He is terminated.

Where does the young lawyer go from here? Assuming he is not prosecuted for fraud, what law firm will hire him? When the lawyer is interviewed for a job and is asked why he left such a prestigious firm, what does he say? Does he call his old employers a bunch of jerks? Or does he say that he wasn't a good fit? Whatever he says, though, in all likelihood a new employer will want a reference from the old firm. What will they say? We all know the answer to that. They will either say nothing, which says everything, or they will tell what occurred. In either instance the young lawyer is not likely to get this job. In bar circles it will be rumored that he was fired for billing hours he didn't work. His reputation will be destroyed. A good life, a life knowing right from wrong and trying to live by that standard, will be lost. (As an aside to this story, in case anyone thinks my example is an unrealistic one, Webster Hubbell, former deputy assistant attorney general in the Clinton administration, went to federal prison for mail fraud for billing hours he didn't work at the Rose law firm in Little Rock.)

Cheating is endemic in many schools. Imagine that you are a senior in college or about to get a graduate degree. Your family is flying in from across the country to witness this wonderful occasion. Their pride in your accomplishment is overwhelming. As graduation nears you are unprepared for the final exam in your most difficult subject. It could be because you haven't studied for it, you had a job that prevented you from devoting the time necessary, or maybe the subject matter is just incomprehensible. We have all been there. The only thing standing between you and your diploma is that one exam. Do you take the harder right and do the best you can, knowing that if you fail you will not graduate and your family will be disappointed? Or do you choose the easier wrong and find a way to cheat? What happens if you take the second path and are caught? The certain consequence is that you fail with dishonor. You and your family will be embarrassed, you will likely be suspended from school or even expelled. There will always be a record of your dishonesty, and the rumors about what you did will follow you for a long time to come. It is a gamble when you choose the easier wrong that your wrongdoing will not be discovered. Even if the dishonesty is not uncovered, it is worth pondering whether this will take you down a slippery slope in life only to be repeated later on the job. (Senator Ted Kennedy to this day is still written about concerning cheating on an exam in college.)

Life may have been going well for Jim at home and in his job. He has two kids in college and a marriage that is okay but no longer exciting. Work is also okay but all too routine. Jim has no real problems other than what he perceives as getting older with no real accomplishments, too many demands on his life, and nothing going on to give him that pizzazz he once had when he was much younger. One day he meets a woman at work. She is a little younger and they seem to have a lot in common. She listens to him with interest, something his wife doesn't do. She seems to care about what he says and is not judgmental. They end up having an affair.

Jim may not be looking to end his marriage at this point. He just wants some excitement, and this affair has brought him that and more. He seems very happy. Jim's wife keeps the checkbook and manages the day-to-day finances, so he has to find a way to pay for his trysts. The costs include hotels, nice dinners, gifts for birthdays, Valentine's, Christmas, and other special occasions. Maybe Jim and his girlfriend devise a ruse to take several days off together to a resort. All of this costs money that Jim can't take without his wife discovering it. So what does he do? The answer is painfully obvious: he steals it from his employer. This is done through submitting fraudulent expense accounts, fraudulent telephone bills, fraudulent travel vouchers, and any other clever way to claim reimbursements that are false and to which he is not entitled. Inevitably the accounting department will figure out the fraud through a variety of detection mechanisms. If Jim is fired for this conduct, where does he go for a job? What does he tell a prospective employer about why he left his present employment, one that he may have been with for many years and where he has risen to a comfortable level? What if the employer decides to turn the misconduct over to prosecutors? Inevitably Jim's life is ruined, his wife will leave him, and the girlfriend will be long gone. His reputation in the neighborhood, community, and elsewhere is gone. So are many of his friends.

There is one word that describes so well how good people can get into trouble—"insidious." Webster's dictionary defines insidious as "seductive"; "having a gradual and cumulative effect"; "developing so gradually as to be well established before becoming apparent." The best way to illustrate this is with some anecdotes from my career. In the previous chapter you read about Larry and how he took money from a vendor "out of an act of kindness" when it was offered, to cover Larry's emergency out-of-town travel. Although Larry reluctantly accepted it, he could easily rationalize it because he fully intended to repay it. It is important to understand that the vendor was someone we would call a prohibited source. That is, the vendor sought to do business with the government agency Larry worked for, and Larry was in a position to influence whether the vendor sold his products.

After Larry returned from his out-of-town emergency he tried to pay back the money to the vendor. The vendor, a master con man if ever there was one to walk the face of the earth, gently declined to accept it. The vendor scoffed in a friendly way at the attempt, suggesting that the amount of money was such a pittance that he shouldn't worry about it. As time went on and the vendor called on Larry just to stay in touch, the two would go to lunch with the vendor always picking up the check. What

Larry didn't understand, and the vendor knew, was that within five years Larry's agency planned a major expansion that would require millions of dollars of equipment that the vendor sold. The vendor was subtly setting the hook for this project years away. As more time went by and Larry and the vendor got to know each other better, the vendor learned of the new church Larry was helping to start. The vendor gave Larry bond coupons to help support this endeavor. It seemed like such a nice gesture. By the time the municipality was ready to bid for the equipment, the vendor had given Larry several hundred thousand dollars.

Larry was a good, decent man. He had a good family and had spent an entire career with his agency. He was well known and respected in the community. On the day he pled guilty to mail fraud in federal court there were television cameras and reporters everywhere. Larry lost everything: his freedom, reputation, pension, health benefits, salary, and friends. At his sentencing a number of people spoke on his behalf describing the virtuous man he had been. Most poignant was the testimony of a middle-aged woman. At her sides were two very deformed young men. They were her sons. She told the judge how her husband had left her when the boys were young, that she had raised them herself, and how it was evident that life had not been easy for her. She went on to say that the one person who was always there, day or night, for her two boys was Larry. Larry would come over on many an occasion when the boys were restless and would not go to bed. He would get them to brush their teeth, read to them, and wait until they fell asleep. I have chosen to believe that this was the real Larry, but in the eyes of the world he will always be remembered as a convicted felon. It was one of the most tragic stories I ever witnessed, all because he failed to recognize how insidious getting into trouble could be, starting with the first small ethical lapse.

I recall talking to a witness, in a case many years ago, who talked about his work environment. The witness was employed by a large company and had a good job with a promising future there. One day an upper level manager came by and asked him if he planned to turn in his expense voucher for the month. The witness said yes, and the manager, being busy, asked if the witness would mind carrying his to the disbursement office, too. The witness noticed that many of the items the manager sought repayment for were fraudulent. The manager had a company car, but he listed subway and taxi charges that the witness knew were false. There were a host of other claims that the witness had reason to know were also made up. At that very moment the witness knew that his boss was corrupt, but in this instance the witness liked the boss. This manager was a kind and considerate person who made life easy for his subordinates. As things turned out, the witness learned that cheating on the company's vouchers was commonplace. It came to seem "okay" to do it since everyone else was doing it.

This young witness was confused and saddened at the same time. He knew that cheating on his voucher was wrong, but there were too many rationalizations that allowed him to engage in it. He had a wife who stayed at home with the children, so his was the only income. He had good benefits and a promising future at a time when the economy was not doing that well. Besides, he worked very hard and wasn't being paid what he was worth. Had he reported the misconduct, including his own, he would have been fired along with many others. The consequences would have been devastating to him. The witness changed jobs for other reasons, but later he learned that there were a slew of terminations at his old company for fraud.

There are several lessons in this case study. One that I think is instrumental to an understanding of getting into trouble is having a boss who sets the tone for dishonesty. When that occurs, it is usually easier to rationalize. It becomes even easier when the boss is a good guy and encourages bad behavior with his own rationalizations. This is a recipe for disaster unless the subordinate has a strong moral and ethical compass and can keep things in perspective. This is when taking the harder right can be incredibly hard—weighing such issues as reporting the misconduct, quitting, and not engaging in it yourself but being ostracized.

Let me recount another important and illustrative case study. It is terrifying and one that I hope the reader will never have to experience. I was at a training in-service, and a former police officer had been invited to speak to our class. The officer had been employed by a major city police department. He was the first in his family to even graduate from high school. The officer told us how proud he had been to graduate from the police academy and how he looked forward to serving the community. Little did he know that his first day in his first assignment would test his ethics and that he would ultimately fail. The officer rode with a more experienced officer who was assigned to break him in. During this first patrol they pulled over a suspected drug dealer. The sergeant had been alerted to appear, too. Two of the other officers searched the car and found drugs and money. Instead of arresting the drug dealer, they let him go without the cash and contraband. The rookie officer was horrified, but it got worse when the others tested him with an offer of some of the money. Here he was, the first day on the job, and he just witnessed his sergeant and two experienced officers engaged in the most flagrant act of corruption.

The other officers explained that the courts were lax on drug dealers, that it was turnstile justice, and that by taking the drugs and money off the street they were doing the community a service. And who better than these centurions should get the drug money? After all, they were all good family people who obeyed the law and would put the money to good use. The rookie told us how he was totally conflicted. But what really made the situation unbearable from the standpoint of doing what was right was observing his sergeant take money. On top of that he was told that money went up to the lieutenant and captain. The rookie officer caved and took some money. After that it was all over as he continued to do it over a period of years. It also became easy to rationalize.

Over time the rookie officer also participated in thefts from stores that had been broken into. When he and other officers responded to an alarm, it was easy to help themselves to some of the merchandise and let the owner worry about it with his insurance company. At some point an internal affairs investigation began, and this rookie and others were caught on film shaking down drug dealers and stealing contraband from their cars. The rookie officer was prosecuted but cooperated and got a deal. However, he lost his job and benefits, he had a felony conviction, and everything he had worked so hard to achieve was gone forever. What makes this story so frightening is the deadly combination of having corrupt bosses all the way up the ladder. In law enforcement this is devastating to the people they are charged with serving. One act of corruption leads to others, and it will invariably get completely out of control. The rookie officer was faced with scorn, possible physical harm, ostracism, harassment, bad work assignments, and more if he took the harder right and reported what he knew to someone outside his immediate command. On the other hand, we know what happened when he chose the easier wrong. For a young impressionable person it can seem like being between a rock and a hard place.

The rookie officer scenario can also happen in the private work place. If a manufacturer is engaged in selling inferior products to save money and boost its stock price, the consequences can be fatal. This is applicable to materials that may go into construction products or that are sold to the military that depends on its munitions to work. If you are a new hire at such a company and at some point discover what is going on, it would appear that there is only one answer (and there should be). However, once again you could be in a situation where you or a family member may have a serious illness, and if you lose your health benefits you face losing your life savings and more.

The different examples discussed here show how good people can get into trouble. There are other pressures that can cause behavioral changes that are out of character, too. They include health problems where there might not be insurance or enough to cover the particular problem. Divorce almost always leads to aberrational behavior because of the strong emotions that are involved. Struggling as a single parent presents all sorts of pressures. Related to divorce are affairs. Sol Wachtler, a then sitting New York State Court of Appeals judge, illustrates this last point. He ended up in prison when he stalked and made bizarre telephone calls to his girlfriend, who had jilted him.

Having an understanding and awareness of the varieties of human behavior that can lead to bad decisions and disaster will serve you well when confronted with situations you never dreamed, or could dream, might happen to you. This book cannot provide specific answers for every situation, but it should make you think.

4 Truth Is Stranger Than Fiction: The Story of Romeo Mike Part I

It was late one afternoon on an autumn day in 1999. A woman walked into a restaurant in south Atlanta. She noticed two men sitting at the counter and thought she recognized one of them as a local politician. She did not dwell on it but merely reacted like most of us who see someone who looks familiar. After the woman began to eat her dinner she noticed something unusual. One of the men handed over a rolled-up newspaper to the other. That person carefully unrolled it and took out a letter-size envelope, which he promptly put into the inside breast pocket of his coat. Shortly afterwards the two men left.

The woman found this activity suspicious in light of her unresolved hunch that the man who received the envelope was a public official. The incident bothered her enough that she reported it to the local district attorney. An investigator obtained the security camera film from the restaurant, but the quality was extremely poor. It showed the two men at a distance, and it showed in a four-second sequence the passing of the newspaper, taking of the envelope, and moving the envelope to the inside coat pocket. The photos were grainy and the faces could not be discerned. After a month or so the district attorney brought the photos to the FBI. An agent was assigned to look into the matter and determine who is in the photos and whether or not there was money or something of value in the envelope for there to be the possibility of a crime.

Another month went by and during this time the photos were enhanced by the engineering unit of the FBI. Despite the effort the quality was still poor. The two men remained unidentified. One day I asked the case agent if he would allow me to show the photos to Romeo Mike, the code name for one of my best sources. I arranged to meet Romeo Mike at a local coffee shop near the FBI office. We sat next to each other in a booth and I handed him a stack of the 8 ½" x 11" photos.

Romeo Mike immediately blurted out several times in a row, "Oh my God, oh my God!" He then identified the two men in the photographs. One was a county commissioner and the other a vendor for the county and other municipalities. Romeo Mike was the chief of staff for the commission chairman of the same board of commissioners, so he knew both individuals quite well. At that moment Romeo Mike knew something that I did not know and would not know until six months later. He knew that his life (as he knew it) had just ended, because he had also taken cash from the same vendor in a rolled-up newspaper. I thanked Romeo Mike for the information and went back to the office to report it to the case agent. Only years later did Romeo Mike tell me in some detail about what was going through his head at that meeting, including shaking so badly when he went to refill his coffee cup that he dropped it.

Six months after this event the county commissioner and vendor pled guilty in federal court to bribery. I was at a debriefing of the vendor, which included his attorney, federal prosecutors, and agents from the IRS. Several hours into the debriefing where the vendor discussed everything he had done and what he knew about others, his lawyer prompted him to tell about Romeo Mike. I could not believe what I was about to hear, that Romeo Mike had engaged in some sort of criminal misconduct. I remembered how we had met in 1995. He had reported to a federal prosecutor with whom he had a passing acquaintance that he thought a lawyer was trying to bribe him and his boss in return for their support of the lawyer, who was trying to sell various insurance products to the county. Romeo Mike worked with me to put together a successful prosecutable case that went to trial and led to conviction of the lawyer. During this time I had gotten to know Romeo Mike and his wife, a young couple, both lawyers, from good families and backgrounds. We developed a relationship that was very useful to the FBI, and during the next four years I enjoyed watching him and his wife have twin daughters born to them. I also took great pleasure in watching Romeo Mike's career advance. He had a stellar reputation and was considered a "go to" person who could get things done. Bureaucratic red tape was not an obstacle for him, and he was good at cutting through it to help constituents. He could also get a phone call returned from the governor.

The vendor recounted his relationship with Romeo Mike and how he had given him money. He said that Romeo Mike had never solicited it, but that over time he was able to get to him. (In Part II of this story, in a later chapter, you will read about some of the factors that the vendor knew to exploit.) The next day the case agent met with Romeo Mike, and Romeo Mike confessed. He retained an attorney and signed an agreement with the government to plead guilty in return for his cooperation and leniency at sentencing. I did not talk to Romeo Mike again until August 2003. During that time he worked with the case agent to identify and gather evidence of other corrupt officials.

Around the second week of August I was packing up and clearing out over twenty-eight years' worth of items. I was retiring on Friday, August 29. The phone rang. It was Romeo Mike. He said that he wanted to apologize for violating the trust that had existed between us and to tell me how much that betrayal hurt him. I assured him that I had moved on, but I talked to him about the grand future I had always seen for him and the sense of loss. Romeo Mike said that he was now divorced and down to his last fifty dollars. He had spent all of his money and retirement funds for daily living and attorneys. He was reduced to making money by mowing lawns and driving neighbors who needed a ride. The thousands of names in his Rolodex had dried up and virtually no one called him or returned a call. He was living wherever he could find a sympathetic heart to give him a room. Romeo Mike talked despairingly of not having even been sentenced to serve his prison sentence, of having no job prospects when he got out, his disbarment, and the daily struggle that he faced and would continue to face after prison.

What I heard in Romeo Mike's voice was desperation and the cry for help from someone at the bottom of the deepest valley. I was very concerned that he was on the edge of looking for a quick but permanent way out. My own father took his life in 1966 when among other things he could not outrun the demons that occupied his mind, and I am sensitive to despair when I hear it. I offered Romeo Mike help if he would accept it, and he said yes. I contacted a local clergyman friend of mine, and he put an associate minister together with Romeo Mike. Coincidentally the two ended up with a lot in common. It was during this conversation that I first broached the idea to Romeo Mike of sharing his story when he got out of prison to alert others to how something like this could happen to them. Today Romeo Mike has a job that pays substantially less than his previous employments. He cannot practice law because he had to surrender his license. He cannot hold a professional license, teach school, or work in any kind of financial institution. His current job comes with no health insurance, retirement plan, sick leave, or vacation. A job with those benefits will have to wait until someone believes in him, as I do, that he is worthy of a second chance in life and gives him a meaningful job.

Romeo Mike is illustrative of a good, moral, honest, ethical person who got into trouble despite all those attributes. Years later after sitting in the coffee shop where Romeo Mike identified the subjects in the photos, I asked him why he did not tell me then that he, too, had taken money and was in a lot of trouble. I told him that had he done so he likely could have worked out a favorable agreement with the government that would have included him going proactive against the two men in the photos. It would have saved the government a lot of time and resources had he done that. Romeo Mike replied that he was so ashamed of what he had done and the breach of trust between us that he couldn't. To his credit, however, he did not call either subject to alert them to an investigation and to give them time to get their stories together. In summation, taking the harder right would have been very hard. Romeo Mike would have lost his job and severely damaged his reputation. He would not have been labeled a felon and gone to prison, though. Choosing the easier wrong was a short-term solution with lifelong consequences. You will read more in Part II about the pressures, temptations, and other things that can skew a person's thinking where he or she will do something so out of the ordinary and life destroying.

5 Character Matters: Fear of Punishment and Hope of Reward

Several years ago I was with a group of people enjoying a cup of coffee during a break and half-heartedly listening to a conversation taking place. A police officer was commenting on an article in the newspaper that day concerning the firing of an officer from another department. According to the story, which I had read earlier that morning and therefore was listening with one ear, a vagrant had been picked up and found with thousands of dollars of cash on his person. The paper recounted how one of the officers decided to supplement his income by relieving the vagrant of some of the money. The chief found out about it, and the officer confessed and was promptly terminated. The police officer retelling this story went on to say that he had trained many rookies in his career and had always instructed them to keep their hands off property that did not belong to them. This was pretty banal advice and so obvious that I didn't pay much attention.

The officer continued to explain why he counseled rookies not to take anything that wasn't theirs: you never knew where there was a hidden camera or microphone to catch you in the act. At that moment I saw the window to this man's soul and knew that I was in the presence of a very bad person.

In another setting I had lunch with a man who was very strong in his religious faith. He was in his early fifties, and he told me how he had never been married and had lived somewhat of an ascetic life as he sought divine guidance each day. The man had had his first sexual encounter in his mid-twenties—with a married woman. Later he was engaged, but there were religious differences that led to their breakup. During our conversation the man was emphatic that he was living his life with the expectation that he would be rewarded in the eternal life. I finally asked him this question: if it was revealed to him with absolute certainty by his God that he had already received his reward, namely having been given life on earth, and that there was no life beyond the grave, would that change the way he lived. The man replied, almost angrily, that he had given up a lot of "good living" with the expectation that it would be rewarded. If there was no heaven in return for all that he had sacrificed it would dramatically alter his life. He continued that he would rob banks and rape women, not only to make up for lost time, but also because there would be no eternal punishment. I saw the window to this man's soul, too, and urged him to continue in his strong religious convictions.

These two stories illustrate the point that anyone motivated to refrain from doing wrong by the fear of punishment or to do good because of the hope of reward is fundamentally an immoral person or worse. No one would question that society needs a police force, not only to investigate crime but to act as a deterrent to those who might otherwise break the law but for the "hidden" presence of a police officer.

Another illustration of this point will help to clarify it. Imagine that you are in a store and the owner has stepped out for a few minutes. There is no one else in the store, located in a rural area where security cameras are not common. The cash register is unlocked. The odds of getting caught stealing the money are almost none. You think about the immediate financial needs that you have and how easy it would be to get away with this. What holds you back, though, is the fear of a hidden camera somewhere despite the odds that there isn't one. You leave without taking the money. Shortly afterwards another customer walks in the store and is confronted with the same situation. This customer, faced with similar financial pressures, thinks about where the owner is out of concern for the security of his cash, never considering the thought of taking what isn't his.

In both instances the result is the same. Neither customer stole the money when the opportunity presented itself. On the surface both appear to be honorable people. However, is there not a difference between the two if you knew their intentions? Surely one would agree that the person who didn't take the money out of fear of getting caught is fundamentally a thief at heart. One acted morally and the other did not, and this goes to the heart of a person's character. If there is any doubt about the difference between the two, would you prefer one or the other individual to live next door to you, or would it matter? You would, and it is because there is a difference. Taking the harder right in difficult circumstances should mean choosing that course because it is the right course, not because of rewards or punishments. The removal of either of these motivating factors could lead to taking the easier wrong with all the attendant consequences. You will read in a subsequent chapter about Diann Cattani, and her story will help to highlight this topic.

6 Life-Changing Versus Life-Shaping Experiences

Almost twenty years ago a friend and I were having a philosophical discussion. He asked me if my Vietnam experience was life-shaping or life-changing. It seemed like an easy question except that I found myself floundering trying to answer it. I told him that I would think about it and try to come up with an answer over a cup of coffee. Well, I thought about it for many years because I am not sure that there is an answer to it, at least not one that would describe everyone who might have shared the same experience. My law-school training taught me to examine issues from many facets, and each time I thought I had figured this one out for myself I ended up thinking of other arguments. Now in my late fifties I have determined the answer for me, and you will have to do the same for yourself. I think that this issue is important because most people will have life-shaping and life-changing experiences. Some will be positive and others will not, but in either instance they will affect your life.

The first issue I wrestled with is determining the difference between the two. It took an Internet search to find one of my former Swift Boat crewmembers. I hadn't spoken with Bob in almost thirty-five years. He had been the engineman and backup machine gunner on PCF 692, and you could not have found a better or more competent seaman. One day, however, he and I were standing outside in the small space between the main cabin and the ocean. He had an M-16 rifle in his hand pointed at the deck. Our conversation was unmemorable. At this point I was completing the last few months of my Vietnam tour of duty and my three-year commitment in the Navy. I had decided many years earlier that I would apply to law school and then to the FBI. Everything was coming together for me.

Suddenly, while I was talking with Bob, he accidentally discharged the rifle. The bullet entered the aluminum deck about a half-inch from my foot and exited the hull of the boat. Needless to say, had it hit my foot it would have completely shattered it, and I would have been physically disqualified from becoming an FBI special agent. I had not thought much about the incident over the years until Bob and I reacquainted by e-mail and he asked if I had remembered it. Instantly I thought about how life-changing it would have been had the bullet and my foot come together. One way of distinguishing between the two terms may be to say that if you have a life-changing event, there is no going back.

I was twenty-three years old with the rank of lieutenant junior grade when I got to Vietnam in September 1969. The Navy entrusted me with a fifty-one-foot boat, a crew of five, and a lot of firepower. I was responsible for the safety and welfare of the crew, navigation, maintenance, and tactical operation of the boat, among other things. I have not had that kind of responsibility since the day I left Vietnam. It was clearly the most life-shaping experience I ever had. My overall Navy experience shaped me for the rest of my life. I learned the importance of character, which encompasses so many different things. And the importance of character is at the core of the message of this book.

Coincidentally, my life-changing experience occurred during my year in Vietnam. The exact date was September 8, 1970. I was in Sydney, Australia, on R and R (rest and relaxation) just before rotating back to the United States. I was visiting an elderly woman named Esther Buck, a retired school teacher. She and my mother had corresponded for more than twenty years by regular mail. They had never spoken because back then a call to Australia would have been prohibitively expensive. It would have also required the intervention of the overseas operator, and such a call could take several hours to connect. My mother and her parents were also teachers, and her parents began a correspondence with Miss Buck sometime in the 1930s through a Parker Pen-pal relationship. My mother picked up the correspondence after her parents got too ill or died.

Miss Buck was very excited to finally meet and talk with someone from my family. She had prepared a nice lunch and began to ask me all sorts of questions. She then asked the question that changed my life forever. To this day the exact wording of it is vague in my mind because it was so shocking to me. What I recall is her asking if my mother had ever reconciled with her parents for marrying outside the faith. The question made no sense to me when it was asked, because my parents were both Protestants, and that is how I responded to it. (At this point my father had been dead for more than four years, after committing suicide.) Miss Buck persisted and said no, no, no, that my mother was Jewish and marrying my father had caused a lot of angst with my mother's parents. My head exploded as I realized the truth of this statement for a variety of reasons. For twenty-four years I had lived with the legend that my father and his family had fled Nazi Germany because they could not support the regime of the Third Reich. For the young man I was then this was a great story, but it was not one I was interested enough in at the time because of all the pursuits the young are usually engaged in, and I was no exception.

I arrived back in New York a few weeks later and confronted my mother with this information. After at first denying it she broke down sobbing and pleaded that I not tell my brothers. She never discussed it again with me despite my repeated attempts over the years. The story went with her to her grave. For me the story just began as I tried to learn more about my family. What I learned over the years from reading and Internet searches, among other things, is that my paternal grandfather was Jewish. My paternal grandmother was a Lutheran, and my father was raised as such. When my mother married him, under Jewish law, she did not marry a Jew because the bloodline is carried down the mother's side. I also learned through a reliable source that my grandfather had some friends in the German SS who were kind enough to give him his only warning to leave immediately or he would be arrested. In 1936 they fled and came to New York, where my grandfather was licensed to practice medicine. I also learned that my father had been very badly beaten by the Nazis, which apparently had affected him the remainder of his life.

There is much more to this story, but I have revealed this much for a reason. I don't see the world the same way that I did before learning that I was a Jew. Although I am not a member of the Jewish faith, I am a part of the Jewish people. I have never seen the world in the same way since September 8, 1970. The discovery of my identity and the pursuit of information of my family history has been nonstop.

Life-shaping and life-changing experiences, as I stated early on, come in various sizes and shapes, but in my opinion it is important to understand the distinctions as they affect you, the reader. In Chapter 3, where I discuss how good people get into trouble, it was the inability to understand this issue that may have resulted in the exercise of poor judgment. When faced with pressures that can adversely influence your thinking under stress, having previously reflected on this topic could make a life-shaping or life-changing difference. A moment of reflection before making a monumental choice could save you from the ordeals you will read about in the chapters that follow. My personal examples are meant only as illustrations. They obviously have no relationship to you but serve as the vehicle to encourage you to think about this subject.

One last example to ponder is the warning about whether your actions would be something you would want to read about on the front page of tomorrow's newspaper. Clearly that could be life-changing, and what you do after that could be life-shaping.

44 *Taking the Harder Right* Life-Changing . . .

7 Going Back to One's Code

Swift Boat training was nine weeks at Mare Island, California. Around the second week my class was flown to the naval facility at Whidbey Island, Washington. This was the most dreaded portion of training: survival school. It was designed to wear you down both mentally and physically. The instructors were allowed, with certain limitations, to hit you, and the only food for the week was what the class members could gather or successfully catch without weapons or fishing equipment. Everything edible had to be divided evenly among the seventy-two sailors in the class. Needless to say it was virtually a week with no food at all. Water was rationed.

The course consisted of some classroom instruction, a map-reading exercise to simulate evading the enemy in the jungle and a prisoner of war (POW) camp. We camped out in the woods each night except for the twenty-four hours we spent in the POW camp, and parachutes were used for sleeping bags. The POW camp phase was the final test of endurance with all sorts of creative stresses brought to bear. The POW camp tested leadership skills and physical and mental stamina after a week without much food and little rest. Leadership was emphasized to the maximum to preserve order and discipline among the ranks, and each of the seventy-two "inmates" had a number based on his rank and date of rank. This was done to ensure that no matter who the guards took out of the prison population, the next person would step up to take charge. One of the mental games the guards played was to entice some of the inmates into betraying other inmates with special favors such as food or cigarettes. Good leadership set high moral and ethical standards for everyone else. The Code of Conduct had been devised because of the complete breakdown of leadership and discipline in the POW camps during the Korean War. Many Americans died unnecessarily because there was no leadership or standards for the prisoners to comport themselves.

The entire survival school course ended when we were all blindfolded and marched once again to engage in some futile exercise that the guards thought of to keep us busy and tired. Suddenly we were told to remove the blindfolds. Standing at attention on top of one of the guard towers was the "enemy" camp commandant. The Star-Spangled Banner started to play and the commandant and all the POWs saluted. It was very emotionally charged, and to this day each time I hear our national anthem I think of that moment. We were then herded to a classroom for a debriefing of the entire week's events. A Navy Commander spoke of the Military Code of Conduct and how adhering to it was instrumental in surviving in a variety of situations, including becoming a POW. The code includes the well-known admonition seen in a myriad of war movies: when questioned, a POW will only provide his name, rank, date of birth, and serial number. Nothing else.

The commander went on to say that there was no record of anyone having ever survived the POW experience who adhered to the "big four" when the enemy interrogators were determined to get certain information. Whether that statement is true or not I have no way to know. It is not even important to the point he was trying to make. The commander said that if the interrogators are determined to get certain information from you, they will. They will crush you mentally and physically until there is nothing left. But when you are mentally and physically defeated and provide prohibited information, and when your beaten and bloody carcass is thrown back into a cell, the commander emphasized in the strongest of words, "You go back to your code." He said that a new dawn will come, and when you are brought back in for additional interrogation you give your name, rank, date of birth, and serial number. Your interrogators will have to work for each factoid as you attempt to live up to the code. This can be very difficult because once someone has broken the code it can seem like a fatal breach of faith. U.S. Senator John McCain, when he was a POW in North Vietnam, was tortured unmercifully until he gave information. He recounted how he wanted to commit suicide because of it, because he could not go back. Fortunately he did not, because he has proven to be an exemplar of "Duty, Honor, Country."

All of us do things that we are ashamed of, embarrassed by, or worse. The essential lesson, though, is that we all have a code that we live by. We know right from wrong and want to do the right thing, but for some of the reasons this book has talked about we stray from that moral compass. That is the time to take hold, recognize what has happened, and go back to your code. It is not too late. You can go back. That is not to say there may not be consequences, but this is where taking the harder right comes into play. (Diann Cattani's chapter addresses this topic in a most personal way.) Someone reading this may be currently engaged in long-time, ongoing misconduct of some sort and thinking, "I have been doing this for so long, it's too late." I can't tell you to take a particular course of corrective action, such as turning yourself in, confessing, etc. For sure I can say that it is not too late to discontinue your destructive behavior. Always return to your code.

8 The Story of Romeo Mike, Part II
Josh Kenyon

Background

Spending my 37th birthday in federal prison was not something that was part of my career plan growing up. It was farthest from it. I grew up in Providence, Rhode Island, and attended an elite private school there. My dad has been a school guidance counselor for years and my mother, before becoming the press secretary to the Mayor of Providence, worked at the private school I attended. My younger brother is a member of the Providence Fire Department. Public service was always an important part of my life growing up, so it is no surprise that I would eventually wind up in public service myself. I did not, however, expect to end up in federal prison one day after pleading guilty to a charge of public corruption.

I graduated from private school in Providence and won an English Speaking Union scholarship to study abroad at a British Public School for a year between high school and college. After studying in Essex, England, for a year I attended Southern Methodist University in Dallas, Texas. I graduated in three years with a triple major in History, Spanish, and Ibero-American Studies. I then went on to graduate from Pepperdine University School of Law in Malibu, California. I met and married my now former wife at Pepperdine; she was also a law student. Her family had moved from her native Ft. Worth to Atlanta, so we decided to move to Atlanta after graduating from Pepperdine.

The move to Atlanta was difficult because Atlanta was still somewhat of an old boys' network city. It had not yet enjoyed the international exposure it would receive from the 1996 Olympic Games, and the legal job market was somewhat stagnant when we moved to Atlanta in the summer of 1992. Since my wife was both a CPA and an attorney, she found a job with a small firm, but I had a more difficult time. Through networking I found a job as a staff attorney with the Southeastern Legal Foundation (SLF), a conservative public interest law firm based in Atlanta. SLF was tangentially involved in politics and through my work I was able to meet many Republican activists, elected officials, and financial supporters.

One of the rising political stars I came in contact with was a young State Representative I'll call "Matthew Stanley." "Matt" had made quite a name for himself in Atlanta for leading a tax revolt that challenged the legality of the mass property re-evaluation in the early 1990s in a populous Georgia county (I'll call it "Center" County, just to be sure of protecting any innocent employees of that government). In 1993 Matt ran in a special election for the position of Chairman of the Center County Board of Commissioners. To almost everyone's surprise, he soundly defeated a famous and highly regarded man to become the first Republican Chairman of that county in decades. Because he was elected in a special election to fill the unexpired term of his predecessor who had resigned to run for higher office, Matt would have to run again in 1994 for a full four-year term.

During the 1994 campaign Matt found himself at odds with some of the county's and state's conservative and Christian activists over his social policy pronouncements. A friend of mine, Pat Gartland, was the de facto leader of the Christian Coalition of Georgia and was called upon by Matt to try to smooth over the uneasiness some of the activists had with Matt's policy statements. During a meeting between the two,

Pat suggested to Matt that he hire someone who had a track record of working with the conservative community in the state and recommended that Matt consider hiring me. I will never forget sitting in my office when Pat called me and asked me if I wanted to work at this important county for Matthew Stanley. At the time I was concerned about taking a position with Matt because some in the Republican Party questioned his character and tactics. I was feeling restless in my job, as I had been with SLF for two years and there was no room for growth in the organization at the time. So when Matt asked me to meet him at the Landmark Diner in Buckhead one October evening I decided to meet with him. Over chocolate milkshakes, Matt offered me a position on his staff beginning in November 1994. I had no idea what I had gotten myself into as I left the safe law firm environment for the world of politics in an important Georgia county and a position on the staff of the likes of Chairman Matt Stanley.

"Center" County

My first position on the Chairman's staff was that of a "policy assistant to the Chairman." In this job I handled constituent complaints about public works issues, press relations, and other matters as assigned. When I joined Matt's staff he was embroiled in a political scandal over the altering of a fellow commissioner's campaign flyer in ways that some interpreted as racist. Matt had initially denied any involvement with mailing the flyer to potential voters, but soon it came out that his campaign was indeed behind the effort. I remember feeling uneasy about working for someone who would engage in such gutter politics and then publicly deny his role until forced to admit it. My intuition told me that I had joined an organization that placed little importance on ethics. This was one of the first instances when I should have listened to my intuition and resigned from Matt's staff.

Within months of my joining Matt's staff, his chief of staff resigned and Matt hired "Mike Best," as I'll call him, a former City of Atlanta Finance Director, to be his new chief of staff. Mike had a reputation for being squeaky clean in an ethical sense and I soon learned that it was justly earned. Mike Best was someone who wouldn't take a free dinner from a potential county vendor and who implored the staff to uphold the highest ethical standards. Mike told us what was expected of us and never ever engaged in below-the-belt politics or gave even the appearance of impropriety.

Soon after Mike joined the staff I noticed that Matt was approaching me to deal directly with me on political issues, occasional issues regarding his personal business dealings, and relations with select county vendors. In other words, Matt was circumventing the chain of command and dealing directly with me without going through or even notifying my direct superior, Mike Best. There were even times when Matt would direct me to not inform Best of what he was asking me to do. One occasion involved Matt's business dealing with a group that proposed building a Department of Family and Children's Services facility in a nearby Georgia county. One of the fellows involved in the deal was someone Best had told me to watch out for, as Best thought him ethically challenged. Matt was aware of Best's dislike for the individual and also believed that Best would find Matt's involvement with the deal ethically questionable. Thus, I was directed to never breathe a word of the business arrangement to Mike Best. This is another example of when my intuition told me something was not right, as I was being told to keep things from my supervisor. Within eight or so months of joining Matt's staff, Mike Best left to take a position with a nearby county. He has never said it explicitly, but I suspect he was uneasy with Matt's style; Best has voiced concerns to me on at least one occasion about the types of people Matt associated with socially and in business. In retrospect, I wish I had left when Mike Best left, as he set such a strong example of right and wrong that I know I never would have ventured down the path I did if Best had been my mentor.

After Mike Best left, Matt asked me to become his chief of staff. I hesitated but accepted and believe to this day Matt wanted me in that position as he knew I was young, twenty-eight, and not likely to challenge him but rather would accommodate him. He was right, as I made it my mission to get the job done and tried to please Matt by doing whatever he asked. Instead of being an advisor I took on the role as a facilitator for someone without a strong moral compass. This led to my eventual downfall.

To understand how someone can go from being sure of his moral grounding to later breaking the law, one must have a sense of the culture of the county. Center County was for sale, plain and simple. Vendors would invite commissioners and staff to lunches, ball games, concerts, lavish dinners at Atlanta's hot spots, and even deep-sea fishing trips. One county staff member even accepted a free cruise from a vendor. At Christmas time it was not unusual to see bottles of liquor being delivered to commissioners' offices from developers and lobbyists. Some commissioners even accepted thousands of dollars worth of Olympic tickets from engineering companies and other vendors. Transportation on private planes owned by people with business ties to the county was not uncommon. Political fundraising from vendors was aggressive. Competition for contracts was not solely based on who was the lowest responsive bidder but based at times on who had done the most for an individual commissioner or group of commissioners.

With this atmosphere at the county offices, it was easy to get caught up in living the vendor-sponsored high life. It started gradually in my case, with vendors inviting me to lunches, then dinners, then sporting events, and so on. No cash changed hands, but plenty of food and beverages and cigars were consumed by me and the many county staff members who joined me on these outings. While there may have been written county policies prohibiting these types of dinners and outings, there was no one enforcing such policies and we were not educated or reminded about such policies. In fact, certain commissioners were at the forefront of engaging in these activities. A lack of firm ethical leadership was evident, in retrospect, and this led to an escalation on the part of vendors as to what they would do to curry favor with county commissioners and staff. A bidding war of sorts was underway for the favor of key county staff members and the implied prize was access to millions of dollars of taxpayer-funded county contracts.

Against this backdrop entered a successful county businessman, who I'll call "George Grange." One day in early 1997, Matt called me into his county office to meet someone he called a supporter and with whom he had a personal business relationship—George Grange. I was introduced to George, an outgoing and likeable fifty-something African American. Matt told George in my presence that he would be out of the office a great deal campaigning for a statewide office and that if George ever needed anything from Matt or his office to contact me directly and I would take care of it. This was somewhat unusual because Matt was basically telling this vendor—in my presence—that I would be instructed to assist him in any way I could. I knew Matt had some sort of business dealings with George but thought it best not to ask about this or bring it up. In other words, I chose to stick my head in the sand and ignore a potential ethical dilemma.

Around this time George's company, which I'll call "Saber Communications," was bidding on some work as a subcontractor to a video-teleconferencing vendor. George called me frequently to ask about the status of the bid and related questions, and I passed him off to another staff member who was spearheading this project for Matt. I had little involvement in this project and was not aware of the specifics, but apparently my attention to George's concerns was inadequate, as Matt told me on at least one occasion that George said I was difficult to get hold of. I believe it was my lack of responsiveness to George on this project that led him to make a now infamous phone call that changed my life forever.

One evening in November 1997 I received a cryptic phone call from George Grange asking me to meet him for coffee at 7:30 the following morning at a local Caribou Coffee shop. I had not had any off-site dealings with George and viewed him as a nuisance rather than a friend at this point. I tolerated him and agreed to meet him only because of his close relationship with Matt. On my way to the meeting, I had second thoughts about meeting him outside of the county offices and felt uneasy with what might transpire. I called Oliver Halle, an FBI Special Agent on the Public Corruption Squad and a personal friend, on my way to meet George. I got his voice mail and said something to the effect that I was on my way to meet a county vendor who gave me the creeps, and I left Oliver a message saying I had a gut feeling that the vendor operated on the fringes and asking Oliver to please call me.

I arrived at the coffee shop and sat down at a corner table with George. He made small talk for a bit about his son who had some recent surgery, and then he got to the point of the meeting. George said that he had several contracts at the county in the works, that he had built some extra money into the contracts, that he would like to call me from time to time to shoot pool or meet at a bar, and that he would be able to "help me out" by giving me an envelope containing $5,000 to $10,000 dollars in cash. I was shocked and dumbfounded. A respected businessman with ties to many of the county's top leaders had come right out and blatantly offered me cash. I sat there in silence for a minute not knowing how to respond. I was scared to say anything as I thought maybe I was being set up and must have looked confused or shell-shocked as George, apparently sensing my nervousness, said, almost as an afterthought, "You know I am helping Matt, too."

Just then, as I heard what I thought was George telling me that he was bribing Matt, my pager went off and the number displayed was Oliver Halle's office number. I thought, "Great, I was just offered a bribe by a county vendor who implied he is bribing my boss and I am getting paged by the FBI all at the same time!" I told George it was good to see him and that we had had an interesting talk, but I carefully avoided specifically mentioning or commenting on his offer. I knew I was not interested in the bribe but was not sure how I was going to handle the matter as it was becoming very complicated.

As I walked out of the Caribou Coffee Shop I was almost in a panic. I sat in my car and called Oliver Halle. When Oliver asked me if I had met the guy this morning and how had it turned out, I downplayed the whole event by telling him that the guy mentioned something about giving me some money but that I believed he was just a big talker. I did not mention any specifics and certainly did not mention that he implied he was giving Matt money. I thought that I could just ignore the situation, not get involved, and it would go away. I never planned on taking any money myself and didn't want to make any allegations about Matt now that he was running for statewide office. Plus, I didn't know for sure that George was paying Matt; that was just what George implied. He could have been bluffing or I could have misunderstood him. Nevertheless, my gut told me that there was something odd about the relationship between Matt and George. My conversation with George basically confirmed the gut feeling that I had that George was too close to Matt. Moreover, it was my opinion, based upon my experience of working for Matt, that George was not the type person Matt would hang out with or be so responsive to if there wasn't something more to it. I had always wondered why such an unlikely pair seemed to be so close at times and now I believed I knew. At this point, in retrospect, I should have taken the harder right and resigned from Matt's staff. I didn't have to rat him or George out, but I could have just resigned and gone quietly away. Two things prevented this in my mind at the time: one was my loyalty to Matt and the second was the fact my wife, Shelly, was out of work.

Shelly and I had bought a house in July 1996 and she had become pregnant in January 1997. We soon found out she was pregnant with twins and, although it was exciting news, it caused some health problems for her, resulting in her being out of work for almost ten months. Naturally, having bought a new house and living on a budget that presumed both of us would be working, her ten months out of work put a financial strain on our young family. The twins were born in October 1997, and I am sure that word was circulating that I was under some financial strain. I have since learned that when someone is in a position such as mine, people talk about you a lot more than you realize, and I had no idea that my personal life was something vendors and fellow county employees gossiped about. I am convinced that one of the reasons George approached me four to six weeks after the birth of the twins was that he perceived me as vulnerable and susceptible to accepting some outside income.

A month or so went by after that conversation at Caribou Coffee, and there was no follow up or mention of the discussion by George or me. Oliver asked about it once, saying if I told him the vendor's name he would follow up on it and at least make a record of it. One day in December or early January, George stopped by my office to chat, and during the course of the conversation he asked if Shelly was able to do any legal work from home as his wife, "Edith," needed some legal work done. George mentioned that it would be a good way for Shelly to make some money and he would rather the money go to us than to some other attorney. I told him that I would ask Shelly about it and if she thought it was something she could do I would have her call Edith directly. Shelly ended up doing $2,800 or so of legal work for Edith but never got around to sending an invoice.

One day in early 1998 George unexpectedly came by my office with a group of BellSouth sales people, and when he walked in he leaned across my desk and handed me some papers. As I opened the papers I noticed an envelope. I was not in a position to open the envelope in front of the BellSouth people and quickly hid it so that no one would notice. I was caught off guard and had no advance warning that he would be bringing me an envelope, so I was a bit concerned as I thought it would look very improper if anyone saw George passing me an envelope. I waited to open it until after our introductory discussion was over and George and the others had left. When I opened the envelope, there was a check for $5,000 enclosed made out to Shelly. Not knowing at the time how much legal work she had done for Edith, I brought the check home that evening and showed it to Shelly. She told me that it was way too much money and that she had done just about half that amount of work. She said she would get around to invoicing Edith but that the check was too much. I took the check back to work with me and the next time I saw George I returned it, saying that it was too much and we couldn't accept it. George said the difference could just be held for future legal work, but I insisted he take it back.

A few weeks later I received a late afternoon call from George asking me to meet him for a drink at a local restaurant that was a popular political hangout after work. The restaurant was right across the street from my office, so I walked over and found George sitting at the bar having a drink with a newspaper folded next to him on the bar. I ordered a beer and we chatted. George got up to leave and pointed to the newspaper and said that there was a good article in it that I might want to read.

When George left I almost didn't open the paper as I customarily read it every morning and didn't think I had missed anything interesting. But sitting there alone drinking a beer, I decided to see if I had in fact missed something. When I opened the newspaper at the bar I noticed a bank envelope in it. I quickly closed the paper worrying that the bartender or someone might have noticed it. I wasn't worried because I intended to take the money but because I was embarrassed that if someone saw, he might think I was taking money. I kept the money in the newspaper and walked back to my office where I counted $5,000 in cash. At this point I still had no intention of keeping the money and kept it in the top drawer of my desk for a couple of days, planning to return it when I next saw George. When Friday came around I took the money home, worried that if someone found it in my office over the weekend they might get the wrong idea and think I was taking bribes. So I took the money home and put it in the top drawer of my dresser, intending to return it. On Saturday Shelly and I went out to eat, and I ran upstairs to get a check to pay the babysitter when we returned home. Instead of getting a check I grabbed a fifty-dollar bill out of the envelope, thinking I would just replace it when I returned the money to George. The money was there and it seemed so easy to "borrow" it temporarily from George. On Monday I found out, when I called his office to see if he was around, that George was out of town for a week or so. I still intended to return the money, but after a week I had taken another fifty dollars out and so on and so on. The next time I saw George I told him he didn't have to do what he did and that it was still too much. He said that he knew I could use some "help" and that he liked me and was more than happy to help out. He never mentioned any contracts or business before the county in that conversation and just passed it off as his wanting to help a friend.

This led me to do something that ended up getting me in a lot of trouble: I rationalized accepting the money. I thought that if

I knew most of it was for legitimate legal work and I declared the whole amount on my taxes then it would be "kosher." I told myself that Shelly had earned some of the money, that the remainder could just be applied to any future legal work she did, and that if I declared the whole amount on my income taxes, how could it be perceived as a bribe? In fact, I was in a policy position at the county, not a management position, and I was not required to complete any annual financial disclosure forms in my position. My position was not one that could award or even vote on the awarding of county contracts. Thus I rationalized accepting the money without ever asking myself why George would so easily part with $5,000. I later realized that what he was buying in his mind was access to my office and the perception that came along with that. He would be perceived by county staff as being connected and in favor with the Chairman because we hung around so much and he could visit my office without an appointment. The truth is I was starting to like George by this point and regard him as a friend, as we did have long talks about life, marriage, and children. The sad thing is he would have had the same access without ever giving me any money, as I had a reputation of having an open door and did give much greater access to vendors I became close friends with, without any thought of any financial benefit to myself. George did not need to pay me the money and I did not need to accept it. The relationship would have been the same, so in the end the payments only led to his and my downfalls.

At the end of 1998 I declared the $5,000 on my taxes and began working for the man who had replaced Matt as Chairman of Center County. I have been teased about declaring what amounted to a bribe on my income taxes. Some of the FBI agents who later worked on my case said I was the first person they had heard of who declared a cash bribe on his federal and state taxes. They joked that the reason cash is given is that it is virtually untraceable unless you do something "stupid" like declaring it on your taxes or depositing it in a bank account. I bring this point up as it is an important part of the story, not to demonstrate my stupidity nor to encourage crafty tax evasion by others. By declaring the money on my taxes I was rationalizing my decision to accept it in the first place. I have since realized that we have an incredible ability to rationalize almost anything and thus do things and continue to do things that we normally would look at as abhorrent.

The year 1999 was probably the second worst year in my life; only 2000 was worse. 1999 was the year I accepted two more payments from George and was separated from and cheated on my wife. Basically, that was the year I slid into the gutter. In April 1999, Matt asked me to accompany him on a trip to Las Vegas with a couple of his friends. Matt and his friends took care of my airfare and hotel room while there, as sort of a gift to me for years of loyal service on his staff. The trip was fun but marked a turn in the road in my personal life that I deeply regret.

Before leaving for Las Vegas I ran into George Grange in the county government building. George told me that he heard from another county employee that I was going to Las Vegas and that he had left something for me in my desk. When I got back to my office I found a bank envelope in the top drawer of my desk with $2,000 inside. George later called me to tell me to "play some numbers for him." I felt odd about accepting the money but took it with me and spent half of it on the trip. By this time George and I were what I considered friends, so I rationalized accepting the money as a gift between friends. Again, no county business was ever mentioned in connection with the giving or acceptance of the money, so I was able to avoid acknowledging to myself that it would still be considered a bribe.

In my personal life I was associating with people who were married but cheating on their wives. Some of the top people at the county who I associated with were having extramarital affairs. So when my marriage was having problems I was surrounded by people who were not influencing me to stay faithful or to try to work things out. On the Las Vegas trip at least one married member of the group I went with spent some time with a prostitute. Another member told me that if I was having problems with my wife I should above all stay married but find some excitement on the side. To this day I don't know what I was thinking or how I could have done what I did, but upon my return from Las Vegas I started hanging out more and more with people who were encouraging me to either cheat on my wife or leave her.

Communication between my wife and me was pretty bad by the end of April and the first part of May 1999. I was working late most nights and going out on the town one to two nights a week after work in spite of the fact that I had beautiful twin daughters at home who were only eighteen months old. So by the end of May I was separated from my wife and dating a fellow county employee. She was twenty-seven or so at the time and recently divorced. She was very outgoing and liked to go out for a night on the town with her friends and mine. She also liked eating out and drinking a good bit, so dating her became fairly expensive.

Once the word got out in the county and among the vendors that I was separated from my wife and seeing someone else, I was inundated with vendors offering me gifts. Looking back I describe it as telegraphing my morals to the community through my actions. Once the various vendors who did business with the county realized that I was willing to date someone while still officially married, they saw it as a sign of weakness in my character that also made them believe I was susceptible to being weak in other ways. One vendor offered me a cell phone to use so I could call my girlfriend without worrying that my wife would get the records from my cell phone if the divorce became ugly. Another vendor offered me use of his mountain home and told me he used it to bring his girlfriend to so his wife wouldn't find out about her. Another vendor who belonged to a private club offered to buy me and my girlfriend dinner at the club whenever I wanted, saying that I could just take her there and eat and drink as much as I wanted and that he would call ahead to cover the tab. Once I displayed a vulnerability or chink in my moral armor, I was stunned with the offers I received from vendors. I didn't accept any of the offers from vendors and was surprised that they were bold enough to make such open offers. Unfortunately, I did not see George as just another vendor and rationalized accepting the cash from him by thinking of him as a friend.

In July 1999 George called me to ask if my girlfriend and I would like to join him and a female friend at a local popular restaurant known for its steaks one evening. Not minding the fact that we were both married, George met my girlfriend and me there one evening for an early dinner. His "friend" was unable to attend. Between the time I separated from my wife and the dinner in question, George and I had become even closer. He was counseling me about my marriage and encouraging me to reconcile even while acknowledging the fact I was seeing someone else. Despite George's own transgressions in the marriage arena, he strongly advised me to try to work things out with my wife and not get divorced. We talked about his divorce and the effect on his children and his own regrets about not trying harder with the mother of his children. During the course of the dinner I went to the men's room to use the facilities and as I was washing my hands George came in and told me that he appreciated my friendship and that he knew I was having a tough time with the separation. He said he wanted to thank me for being a good friend to him and gave me a hug, and while he was doing so he stuck a bank envelope with $7,000 in cash in the inside pocket of my suit jacket. He said he knew I was having a tough time with the separation and wanted to help me out and let me know he was there for me.

We finished our dinner and then my girlfriend and I met some friends at the Steamhouse Lounge for some drinks. I never told anyone about the money George had given me in the men's room. When we got home that night I had trouble getting to sleep as I kept thinking to myself that I had really stepped over the edge and that by accepting so much money from George, I was really on a downward spiral. I thought about returning the money or calling Oliver and turning it over to him. How I wish I had done so and really seriously thought about it. Instead I kept the money and put it and the $2,000 he had previously given me that year on my 1999 income taxes. Again, I thought that by doing so I would insulate myself from any corruption charges if the payments were ever found out.

One thing I did do shortly after accepting the last payment was to make a decision that was a step in the right direction but that was too little too late. I decided that no matter what, I would not accept any more money from George. In the next six or so months George asked me on at least two occasions how I was doing and if I needed anything or any help. I responded each time by telling him that no, I didn't need anything and that I was ok. George later relayed these conversations to the FBI and while telling them that I accepted money he also told them that I had turned him down on several occasions.

I was hoping that by not accepting any more money and by putting in for a transfer to another county office I could get myself out of the bad environment I was in and move on with my life. I had made a decision to change my life and get it back on track, but unfortunately it was too late and the past soon caught up with me.

In late 1999, Oliver Halle called me to ask me to meet him at an Einstein's Coffee House in Atlanta. He asked if I could meet him briefly to see if I could help him with something. What happened next is stranger than fiction. After sitting down and catching up, Oliver asked me if I could look at a few pictures for him and see if I could identify two men in some poor quality photos. Oliver showed me a few photos and instantly my heart sank as I recognized George Grange and Commissioner Michael Higginworth (not their real names) as being the two men in the photos. I quickly and excitedly identified the two men for Oliver, who asked me not to mention the photos or the meeting to anyone. He then excused himself to go to the men's room, and I sat there as my mind raced. Did Oliver know about me and George and was that why he showed me the photos? Was this a chance for me to 'fess up? Was this part of some mind game he was playing with me as he already knew I had taken money? Or was this the beginning of an investigation into George and Commissioner Higginworth and would it ultimately lead to me? Should I ask Oliver for help? Should I go to George and Higginworth and tip them off so we could all get our stories straight? Should I see a lawyer and see if I could cut some type of deal? These were all the things that raced through my head, and I was so nervous that while Oliver was in the men's room I spilled my coffee. I quickly cleaned it up and acted cool when Oliver came back. He and I walked to our cars and he asked me again not to mention the photos to anyone. I told him I was concerned as Shelly had done some legal work for George's wife, but he didn't seem to think that was an issue. Of course I didn't tell him that I was overpaid and that I received two additional payments on top of the overpayment. I decided I would do what Oliver asked and just not tell anyone about the photos and see where it all led.

I will never forget what followed. In April 2000 Special Agent Joe Tucker came to my office to tell me that while I knew that George and Higginworth were being investigated, he wanted to share with me the "good news" that George had decided to cooperate. My heart sank; I knew it was "Game over." Tucker told me that George had told them about the payments to me and that I was under investigation. I promptly told Tucker that George had indeed paid me and that I had declared the money on my income taxes. I then called my friend, Superior Court Judge John Goger, and asked him who he would recommend as an attorney to represent me. He recommended Bruce Morris, who did a fine job representing me. Bruce and I went down to the U.S. Attorney's office the next day, and I signed a cooperation agreement that included me admitting to receiving "corrupt payments." The U.S. Attorney was angry with me as I had the opportunity to 'fess up when Oliver showed me the photos. My attorney advised me to not communicate with Oliver any more as it took him quite a bit of legal maneuvering to keep them from charging me with obstruction of justice as well as corruption. The U.S. Attorney asked that I work with the FBI in helping them build their case against my former boss, Matt Stanley, and directed me to not talk about the investigation until they authorized me to do so. This was mid-April 2000, and they asked me to continue in my job as Chief of Staff to the Chairman until they were ready to have me enter a plea in court. So I continued in my job until June 5, 2000, when I was fired by the Center County chairman after the FBI had questioned him about some of his activities and revealed to him that I had legal "problems." Michael Higginworth entered his guilty plea in front of Federal Judge Richard Story on June 6, 2000, and I followed suit on June 8, 2000.

Continuing in my job for almost two months knowing I had agreed to plead guilty was not easy. I had to act as if I were planning on being with the county for the foreseeable future, all the while knowing my last day could come with just a couple of hours of notice. Commissioner Michael Higginworth was under the same pressure and in the same situation, and it was odd passing by his office just down the hall from mine as we both knew the other was in the same situation, but we were prohibited from talking about it pursuant to our plea agreements.

Something very telling happened about two weeks before we entered our pleas. A local television station, Channel 11, broke the story that Higginworth, Stanley, and I were under investigation by the FBI and U.S. Attorney. Of course the feds had no comment and I denied it pursuant to the plea agreement that directed me to do so. The telling thing was that up until the time the story broke my phone rang off the hook with calls from vendors and fellow Republicans asking for meetings and favors. Once the story broke, however, the calls were reduced to a trickle. I had all these supposed friends, but once they even suspected I was in any type of trouble, instead of offering any support, I was treated like a pariah, ignored, and quickly forgotten. I learned that almost all the people who sucked up to me and acted as if I were a friend were really only interested in me for what I could do for them, and once they thought I was unable to do anything for them they wrote me off. Throughout the whole process I was pleasantly surprised by those who stuck by me and offered moral support and was extremely disappointed by those who did not. There were people in both categories I would have expected to be in the other category, and I really learned who my true friends are as a result of the ordeal.

I ended up waiting to be sentenced until December 2003, over three years after I entered my guilty plea in Federal Court. Michael Higginworth was sentenced and began serving his sentence in 2000 while I was held out by the feds for three years. Even members of the media and some of the FBI agents thought the time I spent with my life on hold was very unfair, given the fact that I had immediately confessed when confronted by Joe Tucker and had agreed to cooperate fully with the investigation. This time in limbo was very difficult, as my life was on hold and I never knew when I would be given just a few weeks notice before going off to prison and did not know how long I would serve.

In December 2003 I was sentenced to six months in federal prison, but I was again in limbo, as I wasn't asked to begin serving my sentence until April 19, 2004. I reported to prison on a Monday, and it was not a fun day. Prison life was boring and reminded me of the movie "Groundhog Day," as every day seemed just like the last with very little variation.

Probably the worst thing about prison was the time away from my children. My twin daughters, Morgan and Eliza, were just six years old when I had to report to the Federal Prison Camp in Montgomery, Alabama, and my ex-wife and I agreed that they would not be put through the ordeal of visiting me there. I complained about the food and about missing them, and in reply I got the note shown on the next page from my daughter Morgan. She writes about wishing she had "the whole summer" with me, about going trick or treating later on, and about sharing "our Christmas" (her spelling is a little creative). That is not, in some ways, the sort of note any father ever wants to get, even though it was wonderful to hear from her and touching to know she missed me. It brought home, in a way that I will certainly never forget, just how painful the consequences of my mistakes were. I had a lot of time to exercise and to think about what got me to the point that I was celebrating my 37th birthday, away from my children, in federal prison.

I realize that I went along with the flow because it was the easy thing to do and that I should have just quit my job when I realized the environment I was in. It would have been the hard thing to do at the time, as I may not have found another job quickly and I had two young children, but it would have been the right thing to do. Instead, I ignored my gut feelings and went along to get along, resulting in a prison sentence. Furthermore, I rationalized my decisions to justify my actions to myself, and I realize now that if one has to go through so many mental calisthenics to feel good about a decision, there is probably something wrong with the decision in the first place.

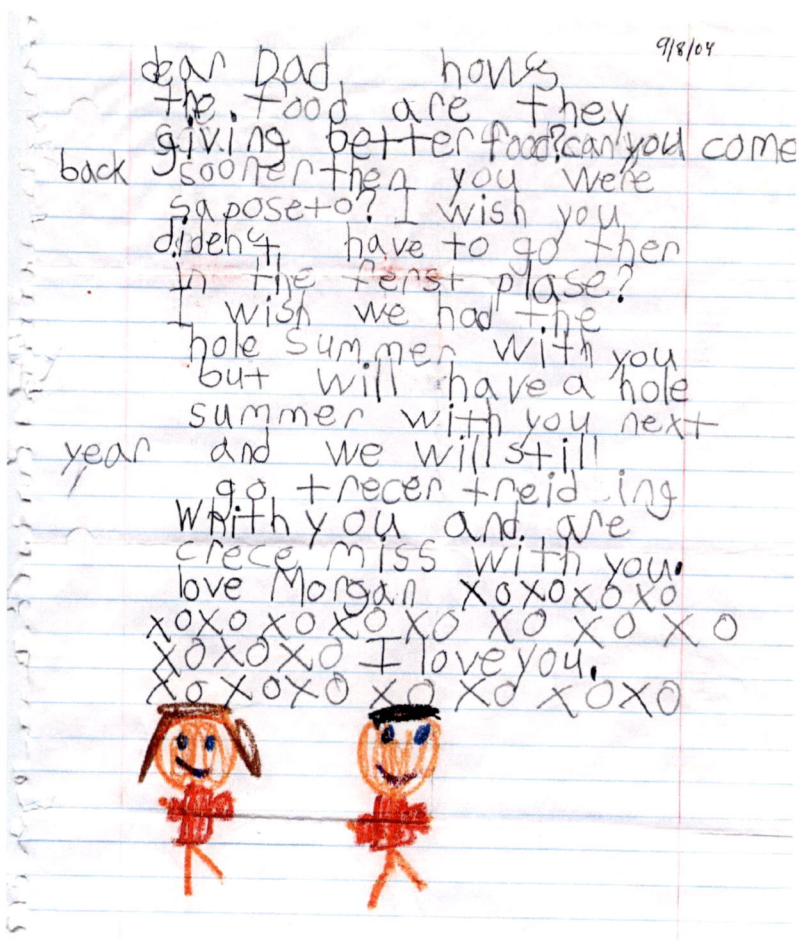

I was released from federal prison on October 15, 2004, after spending what was the slowest six months of my life as "inmate Kenyon." I lost forty-seven pounds in that period, through a combination of not eating much and working out to fight the boredom. Since then I have found gainful employment and have spent a good deal of time with my daughters.

I look back at my actions at the county and it seems like a lifetime ago. I still cannot believe that I ruined such a promising career. While I enjoy my current job, I miss the career that I had prepared my whole life for—public service—and still struggle to forgive myself. It has been less than eighteen months since I was released from prison, and there are days when it seems like I was never there. Then there are other times when I have nightmares about being back in prison. I really do not enjoy sharing my experiences with others, but I force myself to do so, in hopes of reaching someone else who may be in a similar situation. My goal is to motivate that person to change the course of his life after learning about my downfall. If someone, maybe you, can relate to even part of my story and make a change to avert the disastrous consequences I have endured, then maybe my telling my story is worth it. This is difficult for me, but I have a debt to repay for betraying the public trust. My talking about that betrayal to civic groups, students, and professional organizations, and writing openly about it, is one way I think I can help reduce that debt.

9 The Courage to Live
Diann Cattani

Conte Vittorio Alfieri, an Italian poet who lived in the last half of the 1700s, wrote, "Often the test of courage is not to die, but to live." Given the challenges and heartaches of life, it isn't such a stretch to conceptualize the courage it takes to live. The uncertainties in life can be more frightening than the unknown of death—when you're dead, you're dead.

I experienced a time bringing me to this test of courage in living; a time when my hold on life was so tenuous and fearful that the obscurity surrounding death seemed a peaceful alternative, a relief from the tumult, unpredictability, and hopelessness that had become my existence.

It seems almost unfathomable that one could reach this level of despondency without being diagnosed with something terminal or experiencing an unexpected loss of life or some other catastrophic event. As it turns out, living a protected and even privileged life and then facing the unknowns of prison can be one of these catastrophic events having a devastating impact and testing one's courage to live.

I left behind six- and four-year-old daughters and a five-week-old son the day I was ordered to surrender to prison. I pled guilty to stealing close to $500,000 from the company that not only provided me a good salary, benefits, and a meritorious career but that also treated me as family. The crime I committed against the owners of this company is despicable. My children of course are the most innocent and helpless of the victims my betrayal touched, but the ripple effect on countless lives is astounding—it is the very nature of evil.

Albert Schweitzer wrote, in *Civilization and Ethics* (1949), that

> Ethics, too, are nothing but reverence for life. This is what gives me the fundamental principle of morality, namely, that good consists in maintaining, promoting, and enhancing life, and that destroying, injuring, and limiting life are evil.

I had become the example of the evil nature of unethical and even illegal conduct.

I was raised in Preston, Idaho, a small town on the border of Utah and Idaho. In a small town and a large family: I grew up with five brothers and one sister in a strong, loving, supportive Christian home. My parents are the quintessential examples of all that is good. They instilled values of honesty, integrity, love, and selflessness, and they practiced these characteristics seven days a week—they lived as they taught.

As the fourth child out of seven I was no stranger to competition. Each day posed an opportunity for challenges, also known as sibling rivalry. Trying to get bacon before it was gone, the remote control first, the most comfortable chair, the music station you wanted, the shower—most often it was a test simply of agility, but every now and then a brother could be outwitted.

I attribute the reason sports came so naturally to me to this "friendly competition." Living in a small community, there was ample opportunity to participate in organized, competitive school-sponsored activities. I ran track and played softball, basketball, and volleyball, and I'm quite certain I could have suited up and made the football team—with five brothers I took a few hits and throwing "like a girl" was not acceptable, not even in the back yard.

I excelled in volleyball and our high school team performed well, becoming state volleyball champions and putting us all in the spotlight. I was fortunate to catch the eye of several college scouts, and I was recruited by a number of universities and eventually decided to accept a scholarship from Brigham Young University. The volleyball program at BYU was exceptional during these years, consistently ranked in the NCAA top ten of Division IA schools; and BYU had not only an outstanding sports program but also a top-rated academics curriculum.

I studied business management and psychology at BYU in addition to year-round sports, and after leaving I had a burning desire to experience a less disciplined kind of action—the action of a big city. I moved to Atlanta because it was a long way from Utah. It appealed to me as a single woman. Action, opportunity, and diversity—these were the things I felt I'd missed growing up in a small town, attending a private university, and conforming to the regimen of intercollegiate sports. I was ready for reckless abandonment of the suppressed environment I'd been surrounded by. I appreciated my opportunities, but although everyone's beliefs and values had varying degrees of personal interpretation, overall it seemed that everyone was the same and was expected to act the same.

When I moved to Atlanta I threw myself into the social opportunities of a large city—there was so much to do. I belonged to the Atlanta Snow Ski Club and the Atlanta Water Ski Club, and I began cycling—both road racing and mountain-bike racing. I lived a very active lifestyle, was surrounded by more temptation than I could imagine, flirted with these temptations on the edges, but I was still able to hold fast to the solid values practiced in my home.

I worked a couple of jobs that were fun, little more than hobbies before getting serious about a career. I was eventually offered a position with a "boutique" (small and specialized) human resources consulting firm. Shortly after beginning my career, I met and married one of the few Atlanta natives. Between opportunity through BYU, individuals I met through various organized clubs, and our two careers I was afforded a variety of unique and prestigious opportunities at a very young age.

I have had dinner at the White House and dinner with George and Barbara Bush in Maui, Hawaii. I've been to dinners and ceremonies at the Georgia governor's mansion and attended parties and weddings in the company of numerous famous politicians and business leaders.

I've watched the Braves lose many World Series games sitting in the box next to Atlanta Braves General Manager John Schuerholz—not an ideal location to enjoy a game when that much money is at stake.

I've flown on private jets and corporate jets, and I've attended sporting events in the company of some of Hollywood's most elite. I've stayed in the homes of CEOs and been a repeated invitee to the Blockbuster Entertainment Awards.

I've had the opportunity to facilitate leadership development, team building, and diversity training courses, and I have worked alongside executives in not only many Fortune 500 companies but also in government and in privately held companies in a variety of industries. Looking back on these experiences with more mature eyes, I see with clarity the ethical and unethical individuals and companies I've been exposed to. I worked with and observed leaders who lead with passion, vision, and well-defined values, their professional behavior consistent with their personal behavior. I have seen leaders in corporations and government who articulate certain standards in the boardroom and act in direct conflict with these standards in the "bar room." I have witnessed those who vacillate depending on the personal reward or gain—never once considering the impact on the masses. And I've been with those who would never consider deviating from their moral code regardless of individual consequences or rewards.

Had I stopped to contemplate the quality of my life, interactions, and associations, I would have been forced to make some tough choices; instead I was focused on the glamour and prestige—the "headiness" of the experience and unconcerned with ethical or moral issues. I was embracing "life in the fast lane," the rush that was feeding into a significant ego trip, ultimately having catastrophic results and eventually the loss of all dignity.

Instead of being haunted by volleyball serves missed in the "Final Four" NCAA championships—instead of such ephemeral sources of pain, I'm haunted, tortured in fact, by being served up (or serving myself) all of these: guilt; attorneys; courtrooms; consequences; and the devastating effect my crime has had on former employers, my children, family, friends, colleagues, and clients.

I was an honor student and all-American athlete, raised in a world of black-and-white moral certainty, and had a privileged upbringing. I was surrounded by love, security, and opportunity; I had a meritorious career, dined with Presidents and CEOs; I had a husband and children—I had *everything* going for me. But I moved to fingerprints, mug shots, strip searches, and living, eating, sleeping, and living in—even sharing—what I once had considered a substandard walk-in closet. How? Why? These questions probably still haunt many.

The human resources firm I worked for was very small, and I was initially hired to manage a large-scale project with Blockbuster Entertainment to implement a hiring process and develop a personality profile, identifying characteristics of strong performing store and district managers throughout the country. The project was in its embryonic stages, so in the interim I began setting up the business—automating their bookkeeping system, interviewing and contracting payroll services, implementing benefits packages, securing vendors, researching information technology companies, working with independent programmers, interfacing with the accountants and lawyers, and managing related processes.

I demonstrated a significant amount of diligence, competency, and loyalty during this period, and the owners felt it would be advantageous to them to leave these functions under my control, freeing them for travel and continued business development. As the project grew I moved into a more consultative role, and all this meant hiring additional staff to maintain the fundamental, daily transactional functions. I maintained overall accountability of accounts payable, accounts receivable, collections, taxes, insurance, benefits, legal issues, and related matters.

No one directed me to implement any internal controls or operating procedures. I did not omit doing so, or set up any relationships, with the intention to steal—I wasn't taught how to steal in my home or school—I didn't know how; but with opportunity, I learned. My deception started innocuously. We were flying to Utah for the Christmas holidays, and shortly before leaving I noticed the travel agency had made an error in charging the trip to my corporate American Express account. Things were hectic before leaving and I didn't get around to calling the travel agent to re-issue the tickets, but I planned to reimburse the company when I returned. It was all quite harmless at the time, but months went by and I didn't reimburse the company; I rationalized this indiscretion by telling myself it was more of a business trip than vacation anyway. I had to check voice mail, e-mail, take calls from staff, interact with clients, and participate in conference calls—so where was my "vacation"?

Many in business and especially in the industry of fraud and accounting, people like Certified Public Accountants (CPAs) or Certified Fraud Examiners (CFEs) are familiar with what is known as the "Fraud Triangle—Opportunity, Pressure, Rationalization." All three sides of this triangle were coming into play in my life, feeding off each other in a vicious cycle.

The opportunity had always been there: I basically set up the business infrastructure of the company. I determined who got paid; signed checks; reconciled the bank statement; called in payroll; signed public relations checks and reconciled public relations accounts; ran monthly, quarterly, and yearly reports; calculated bonuses; interacted with the accountants and attorneys; and reported to the owner. I set up the whole system—it was mine. I solely determined what and how all information was disseminated to various individuals.

Career pressure was mounting as the business grew—accounts were becoming more numerous as we added vendors, subcontractors, temporary help, information technology support, college interns, and others; we were moving into more executive coaching and team building. Along with the leadership training and Blockbuster project, the business was becoming more labor-intensive and stressful as I continued to travel and facilitate programs.

Being part of a small or "boutique" firm brings with it the expectation of having to wear numerous hats at different times; mine were all becoming extremely heavy, time-consuming, and cumbersome. Compounding the career pressure was the personal pressure. I was pregnant and would be having my first child at the beginning of February. This would mean a significant shift in job structure, taking me off the road, reducing my income, and contributing to anticipated financial pressure. Being in front of people was also the most gratifying aspect of my career, and I would soon be moving to working more from home and the office.

Our peer group had consisted of millionaires since the time I was in my mid-twenties and although my husband and I made an enviable combined income, by comparison it never seemed like enough. I never stopped to consider who I was comparing myself to and the ages of those I was comparing myself to but instead felt I needed to measure up, adding a self-imposed pressure of "keeping up with the Joneses." How was I going to make even less and still maintain a lifestyle I liked and didn't want to sacrifice?

After our daughter was born life as I knew it changed drastically. My husband was still working long hours, traveling endlessly, and I was being pulled by the social aspects of his position, struggling to stay on top of my responsibilities/career and also to be the "perfect" mom. I didn't want to give anything up; I wanted it all. Greed, selfishness, and unthinking devotion to a lifestyle were paramount in contributing to my crime. We were spending a significant amount of money on babysitters because of the social demands of my husband's career, my career, and our personal relationships. The financial pressure was increasing and the extra money needed seemed easy enough to rationalize. Certainly the company should be paying for a babysitter, gas, and meals. There should be *some* trade-off for my twenty-four-hours-a-day, seven-days-a-week availability.

I was working out of my home more, and that of course required a state-of-the-art office, equipped with the most recent technological "must haves"—compliments of my company. As the company grew we needed additional office space so we renegotiated leases and exercised build-out options. The company purchased desks, chairs, artwork, all of which I handled—some for the company and some for myself.

There were times the owners would be snowed in at the airport in the Northeast and I was called to go to their home late at night to feed and let out the dog. The dog disliked me and I disliked the dog—we battled for hours. This type of "inconvenience" certainly demanded extra hours, extra pay, and a tank of gas. Or so I rationalized. At times their children needed things like deposits made when their parents were traveling or needed to borrow my SUV to move—all of these things fed my sense of justification for padding expenses and using company credit for gas, meals, and personal travel.

The opportunities to steal were numerous and I seized them in countless ways—I reimbursed myself from physical receipts, and when the credit card statement came in, I reimbursed myself again for the same items. Of course each time there was corresponding documentation. I created "dummy" invoices and paid myself; I paid personal credit card accounts with company checks and initiated other forms of deceit and criminal subterfuge. I literally controlled all accounts and decided what information was shared.

The ability I had to rationalize and compartmentalize my deceit was scary. Not only was I able to justify my crime to myself, but I was also able to conceal it and internally minimize it to the point that it didn't seem like I'd taken much money anyway. I had "earned it," and "I deserved it." The mind as a whole is extremely powerful and I was using it to the destruction of not only myself but many others. However, up to this point I still couldn't (or wouldn't) see it. I believe we all have the ability to rationalize, deny, and compartmentalize, to tell ourselves lies to the point we can no longer differentiate fact from fiction. The difference is in our ability to control this power, exercise restraint, and use it for good.

I had always thought of myself as an honest, ethical person—I was brought up that way—but there was a serious crack in my foundation. When put to a long-term test I failed. Each time I initiated my duplicity I would tell myself that this was the last time; I would pay it back, there would be no more. Unfortunately greed had become a more potent motivator than my conscience, which on some level had become almost nonexistent.

Temptation is insidious by nature—almost always beginning small and unobtrusive, but once the line is crossed and corrective action is not taken, it becomes easier to do again until the line is blurred and eventually ceases to exist. My line ceased to exist. My life continued to unravel as career, personal, and financial pressure mounted and it was becoming increasingly difficult to compartmentalize my criminal activity. I no longer knew who I was and which face was the appropriate one to put on at different times—I was constantly on edge and anxious. I now had two children, an absentee husband, a crumbling marriage, and it was becoming impossible to separate my deceit from my everyday interactions.

I began to get sick often, was unable to sleep, and experienced severe night sweats. I sought out several specialists, expecting to be told I had a "terminal" disease, but every test came back normal. Subconsciously I knew my physical manifestations were most likely symptomatic of the stress of living a dual life, and this was one of the contributing factors leading to my subsequent confession.

The impetus that led me to finally take the "harder right" and show up at the owners' office to confess was when I was at my home one day with the "Oprah" television program on in the background—I remember the day as if it were yesterday—February 12, 2000. I was only half tuned in to the program and even today I don't know the "secret" the guest was protecting, but I remember hearing Oprah as clearly as if she had come into my own family room say to this woman, "You cannot be a complete person with this secret." "You cannot be a whole mother to your children carrying this burden." She might as well have been speaking to me, because I crumbled at the realization that the one thing I truly valued the most was my love and caring for my children and they were being cheated out of a healthy mother. I had one choice and that was to confess.

My confession resulted in a string of sessions with civil and criminal attorneys, meetings with the FBI, defense attorneys, federal prosecutors, investigations, audits, paperwork, accusations, insinuations, and court dates—civil and criminal. Having to admit to such embarrassing and despicable behavior to people who loved, respected, and believed in me is a humiliation difficult to describe. My mother had just recently retired, and my parents had always had a goal of serving a mission for our church when they retired. This was their time, but the decision to go wasn't so clear anymore. The family consensus was they should move forward with their dream and that with siblings and in-laws, the support would be available as I moved through the long and tedious system. If necessary, they would come back and offer whatever emotional and financial support they could.

My parents were called to a humanitarian mission in Istanbul, Turkey. The children and I flew to Utah to join my entire family as my parents prepared to depart. My husband dropped us off at the airport, but when we returned a week later my husband wasn't at the airport to pick us up. I called every number I knew searching for him, to no avail. My ATM card was rejected when I tried to get cash for a cab. Fortunately my dad had given me, as he has all my life, some "travel money" and I was able to pull together enough cash to get us home. When we finally arrived home my daughters went in as I was getting our bags and came out screaming that we'd been robbed. I ran into the house and immediately knew we were not robbed by a stranger. Then I found the divorce papers on the counter. The accounts had been closed, the money to live on was gone, and I was devastated. I then found myself simultaneously in civil court, criminal court, and divorce court fighting not to lose custody of the children I had basically raised to this point. The clincher yet to be discovered was that I was pregnant.

There are what is referred to as life-shaping and life-changing events. I was still learning the difference and it wasn't until the end that I came to understand that there is a clear delineation between the two. Everything to this point was shaping my life, my thinking, and my learning.

Six-months pregnant, I stood in Federal Court and was sentenced to eighteen months in federal prison. I was nine months pregnant the day I stood in Superior Court and my divorce was finalized; three days later my baby was delivered and five weeks post-partum I was ordered to report to prison. That was the day that *changed* "me"; that day redefined my life, my views, my commitment, how I see others, how I interpret situations, and the choices I will make, forever.

After spending fourteen months in Turkey, my parents cut their mission short four months early to move to Atlanta to take me to prison and to remain in Atlanta during my incarceration to help with the children and to insure I could see my children on visitation days. I went to my four-year-old daughter's pre-school Thanksgiving program and then hugged her goodbye. I went to my six-year-old daughter's first grade class, where I hugged and kissed her goodbye. I held my son the entire five-hour drive to the Florida prison where I was assigned.

Anyone who knows me realizes that I am notoriously late, and reporting to prison was no different. I was late and the individuals conducting the "intake" were quite angry. I remember thinking how odd to actually expect people to report to prison "early," but apparently this is expected. I handed my baby to my mom as I was whisked away to be "processed" into the system. I was trying to control the myriad of emotions and draw on my past ability to compartmentalize, thinking I would be able to complete my sentence, block it out, and eventually go on with my life, pretending it never happened.

Once again I was stripped of dignity and literally stripped as well. I was searched, fingerprinted, deprived of all personal belongings, and issued my prison clothing, bedroll, and ID. I was no longer "Diann Cattani"; I was now "53668-019." An officer led me down a long hallway with windows lining each side. Through one wall of windows I could see into the "compound" and observe the "population"; running parallel on the opposite side I could see into the administrative lobby where I had come in. My parents were still in this area, watching for me—my mother hugging my baby with tears streaming down her face. My dad, a man I idolize, a man of deep but rarely displayed love and emotion, was standing with one arm around my mother and with his shoulders convulsing. Quiet tears streaked his face. I wanted to run to them, I wanted to run from them, I wanted to scream, I wanted to fall on my knees and cry as I saw the excruciating pain they were in because of me. There was no one to blame and nowhere to look but inside.

I knew at that moment I would not block this experience out but that it would be interwoven into the person I would become and I owed it to many people to rise from this self-inflicted tragedy and make something of myself. Almost as scary as the prison environment is the actual time available to reflect and evaluate your life—the words of Socrates (469-399 BCE) came to mind: "The unexamined life is not worth living." This was my time to examine my life and I was not going to let fear stop me.

I was a minority in the system—I was white, my crime was white-collar, by comparison with others around me, my sentence was very short. I was educated, and I had a supportive family with the means to provide for my needs while incarcerated; I had all my teeth and apparently I was one of the few in the system actually guilty. (It's amazing how many people in prison were "framed.") I also told on myself, not something that commands respect from fellow inmates.

Prison is no Club Fed—I learned that survival meant learning and following hundreds of rules administered by the Bureau of Prisons. Just as important to survival, I learned, are the hundreds of rules issued and enforced by the inmates, the "population." Oftentimes these two sets of rules were in direct conflict with one another, imposing a fine line to be walked because it was imperative that all rules were followed. The experience was nothing short of a nightmare.

Prison is no place to learn right from wrong. It is not the place to define your values and establish a moral code to live by. I was an anomaly in the system and grateful to be one, but it was also frightening not to "fit in." It didn't take many hours in prison to realize how fortunate I was and how unremarkable my story really is—all around me women were faced with things like (often several of) these: divorce; abandonment by family, spouse, and significant others; children taken into state custody or by family members, leaving the inmates with no legal rights; homes foreclosed on and cars repossessed; death or sickness of loved ones, with inmates unable to grieve or to help; sickness of the women themselves; and financial and personal chaos. The sights, the sounds, the smells surrounding me left me physically ill. Emotionally I felt varying degrees of shame, guilt, anger, fear, remorse, and an overall sense of hopelessness.

Writing had become my greatest catharsis during the two years leading up to prison; the entry following my first few hours in prison is something I occasionally reflect on:

> As I sit here I have a choice—I can choose to sit in a perpetual state of sadness and self-pity immobilized by the gravity of what I've done and my current situation or I can make the choice to rise from the guilt and pain. Even in this place I still have the greatest gifts available to me—my life, my health, and my family. I choose to rise above this and become better and not bitter.

I was very fortunate to have the love and support of my family. It didn't take more than a couple of stories from others to understand just how auspicious that was. My family was able to bring my children to see me regularly—they had the financial means to support me in getting the things I needed, items from the commissary to make prison life more bearable. They were able to send enough money to pay the astronomical telephone charges required to speak with my children each day. The sacrifices made on my behalf were remarkable.

This ripple effect my actions had on so many is explained very eloquently by the poet and divine John Donne in his classic *Devotions upon Emergent Occasions* (1624):

> No man is an island, entire of itself; every man is a piece of the continent, a part of the main. If a clod be washed away by the sea, Europe is the less, as well as if a promontory were, as well as if a manor of thy friends or of thine own were. Any man's death diminishes me, because I am involved in mankind and therefore never send to know for whom the bell tolls—it tolls for thee.

I've come to understand and internalize this in a very personal way—we are interdependent components of a whole and our choices affect others—positively or negatively, we decide. There is no right way to do wrong. The lessons I have learned, and learned very much the hard way, are:

- If you find yourself rationalizing a decision or action, re-evaluate because it is probably wrong.

- Listen to your gut and follow it.

- Define what you want to stand for, and most important, evaluate your actions frequently.

- When (not if) you deviate, make an immediate correction—take the harder right. The consequences are less devastating and the quality of your life will improve.

- Find a mentor; don't try to handle the pressures of life or business alone.

There was a time I would have looked at someone like me and thought, "This person is twisted." I thought it could never happen to me, but I was wrong. It can happen to anyone who is not prepared in advance to face the challenges and choices of business and life.

Today I go forward labeled "felon" and, for the rest of my life, this has many ramifications. Each day I have to look in the mirror and remind myself that I committed a felony, but that I am more than the sum total of my mistakes. I have lost everything of financial value: job, career, home, car, savings, retirement, and benefits; but more important even than any of those things, it cost me my freedom—time and experiences with my children and my family I can never get back.

The consequences will be felt forever by anyone close to me. WSB-TV, Atlanta's ABC affiliate, covered my story and our **Taking The Harder Right** seminar. When Dale Cardwell, the reporter, notified us it would be appearing on the news, I had mixed emotions about watching it. I've endeavored to be as candid with my children as I felt appropriate for their ages from the time I turned myself in, and preparing them for this coverage was no different. However, as much as you try to prepare someone for something unpleasant, you can't tell them what to feel or expect on an emotional level. As my now eight- and six-year old daughters sat down to watch their mom on TV there was significant anticipation. The anchors did a lead-in of my story complete with my picture, then went to commercial.

My six-year-old daughter ran into her bedroom, threw herself on the bed and refused to come out to see the actual story. My eight-year-old daughter and I watched the brief coverage and, in her enthusiasm at my "fame," she immediately wanted to call her friends to tell them her mom was on TV. I slowed her down and reminded her she would also have to explain "why" mom was on the news and she was obviously very deflated at realizing it wasn't something she could be proud in bragging about. I went into the bedroom to talk with my six-year-old and she was not only angry but also tearful. As I probed to identify what was so upsetting, she said she didn't like seeing my picture on TV; it reminded her of me being gone, of missing me, of crying at night, not being able to hug me, or talk to me, having to drive in the car on the weekends, and getting carsick each trip. She also said it made her scared I would go away again. I will never go away again, but I can't make up for having been gone.

People act immorally, unethically, and often illegally every day—they may never "get caught," making it appear enticing, glamorous, easy, the only way to get ahead; I don't believe you can operate in shades of "unethical gray" without eventually crossing the line into illegal activity. Whether or not these individuals are ever caught is irrelevant—they aren't free. Freedom is more than a physical state; freedom is acting in accordance with a strong moral and ethical value system; enhancing and promoting life, which ultimately results in freedom of conscience—internal peace.

Former Speaker of the U.S. House of Representatives Newt Gingrich recently said, "You can't have a corrupt lobbyist unless you have a corrupt member [of Congress] or a corrupt staff. This was a team effort" (Associated Press, 5 January 2006). All of us, whether in business or government or elsewhere, have to keep in mind that leaders in organizations set the standard for ethical behavior. A culture of honesty has to be maintained by organizational leaders and sustained by individuals who consciously strive to uphold, and when necessary to return to, the highest moral code.

I share this humiliating story about myself in hopes of playing a small role in encouraging individuals to monitor their moral compass; to say something that might touch someone who is flirting with shades of gray to have the courage to live well and do their part in contributing to a culture of integrity.

Thomas Jefferson said, "I like the dreams of the future better than the history of the past." I do, too. I'm not proud of my "history," but I still have everything of real value—my life, my health, and my family. I must believe I have every reason to dream and know my dreams and goals are attainable with perseverance. Using opportunities to share my story in hopes it might resonate with someone; holding myself up as an example of what not to do; raising the level of cognizance to the consequences of our decisions and the impact our choices have on others and acting as a conscience and guide for people navigating their own inevitable ethical dilemmas—these are my goals. Being a part of ***Taking The Harder Right*** fulfills one of my dreams. With honesty and hard work, dreams can come true.

10 From Ambitious and Upwardly Mobile to Miserable and Broke in Under a Decade
Walt Pavlo

MCI Telecommunications, Inc. (1992-1997)

In May 1992 I began working for MCI Telecommunications in Atlanta, Georgia. I was excited to work for this relatively young company, founded as the mother of modern deregulation in telecommunications. There was no more exciting industry in the 1990s than the fast-paced and ever-changing world of telecommunications.

I graduated with a degree in Industrial Engineering from West Virginia University in 1985 and earned an MBA from Mercer University in 1991 as part of their executive MBA program. My jump to MCI represented another accomplishment in a string of finance positions that I had held at Goodyear Aerospace and GEC Avionics, Inc. The position at MCI would provide me with my first management experience, at the age of twenty-nine, in the collections department for carrier services.

A position in collections was not my first choice of jobs, nor did it make me especially proud. Having the position at MCI did. As I bragged to friends, I would be a manager for collections of customer accounts that represented carriers of long distance who purchased long distance services from MCI and resold it under their own brand name. Customers with names like Global Crossing, WorldCom, Qwest and others made up the base of prestigious client names that were posting records for growth and earnings.

I thought of myself in 1992 as a decent, honest, moral guy. As far as I know, my friends then, my wife, my relatives all saw me the same way. I was not only trained in management skills, I was also educated and I certainly knew right from wrong. I was raised right. Everyone who knew me then, including me, expected me to go pretty far, to amount to something, to succeed. All of us expected me to earn a good living and to make it in a way that would earn and keep the respect of those around me. No one, especially not me, foresaw that in less than ten years, I would go to federal prison. Or that prison would be followed by a halfway house and then by a frantic, excruciating fight to regain my livelihood, my self-respect, and a return to the general esteem of others that I used to take for granted.

Mine is not a story of evil arising from nowhere, but it is also not a story of a man's own evil nature finally being discovered. My story is in most senses pretty ordinary, fairly predictable. But it includes emotional pain I wouldn't wish on a truly evil person, and it includes a hell of a struggle to realize that I brought the pain on myself, that I deserved the pain, but that, finally, I deserve to move on to better days.

Not only did MCI in 1992 mean prestige, it involved huge sums of money. The carrier business segment had an accounts receivable base of approximately two hundred fifty million dollars each month during 1992. Most of these balances represented just a few of the over 1,000 customers that came to MCI for the purposes of reselling long distance. Giant telecommunication companies like Sprint, AT&T, and WorldCom came to MCI to buy long distance to supplement their own growing networks. Other startup telecommunication companies came to MCI because it was the only network that they had. For many customers, MCI's network was their network as well, and they paid handsomely to be a part of it.

As with most business models, volume and relationship with MCI had an impact on pricing. It was no different in telecommunications. MCI had a large network that had been paid for with billions of dollars raised from stock and bond offerings. The result, like that of other telecommunication companies, was an overbuilding of network capacity with the hopes that one day it would be filled with phone, video, text, data, voice, and Internet services. MCI used less than 50 percent of network capacity for my entire time at the company. So what to do with an underused network? Sell it to your competitors.

Competitors like AT&T, Sprint, and WorldCom had their own networks, but they needed MCI's to supplement their own. MCI purchased long distance services from these companies as well. With this strange business model, two forces were at work to drive down pricing, and therefore profits, with these types of customers: 1) large volume purchases in the tens of millions of dollars each month and 2) MCI's inclination to give better pricing to customers who were also selling telecommunication services to MCI. Because of these forces, MCI had a strained, and not very profitable, relationship with some of the top names in telecommunications, but at the same time those same names represented nearly 80 percent of the revenue for the business segment. So the question became, where do we get profits in this business segment? The answer was a group called "Tier 3" Carriers.

Throughout the 1990s, telecommunication carriers were sprouting up all over the country. Each of these had a niche that catered to a certain type of service, feature, or clientele. There were carriers who specialized in prepaid calling cards, 900 services (including pornography, gambling, and fortune telling services), deeply discounted long distance services, and growing Internet services.

After MCI's historic battle that broke up Ma Bell, deregulation was embraced and free market competition was seen as the best way to benefit consumers and expand technology. The barriers to get into the long distance business were very low and capital requirements were minimal. There were few technical barriers either for many new carriers, as large companies like MCI provided much of the technical expertise necessary to get a small company up, running, and using MCI's long distance. Everyone lent a helping hand to many of these small companies and MCI particularly embraced the wholesale market. After all, MCI itself was "one of them" and AT&T was seen as the true enemy of all carriers of long distance, even after the breakup.

MCI enjoyed tremendous revenue growth as companies like Sprint, WorldCom, Frontier, Qwest, and many other companies continued to grow their business base. From 1992 to 1995, the accounts receivable base that I collected on grew from two hundred fifty million dollars each month to over one billion dollars each month. Most of the revenue came from good paying customers, with a smaller amount coming from Tier 3 customers.

Tier 3 customer profiles tended to all look the same. Their owners had little technical expertise, their business model was based on revenue achievement goals, their financials were weak, they were highly leveraged with little working capital, and they rarely paid their MCI invoices in a timely fashion.

MCI needed Tier 3 customers because they represented the majority of profits for the business segment. They were usually selling in retail environments, where they could afford to pay a premium for long distance because the unique aspects of their retail products (like 900 services and prepaid calling cards) allowed these products to be sold at premium prices. At the end of 1994, MCI had a number of such carriers on its network and aggressively went after others throughout 1995.

But with added profits came added risks. Risk for MCI could be defined then as the chance that a customer would default on its payments to MCI.

During 1995, I was assigned to travel the country to negotiate payment plans and recovery plans for customers who had fallen behind on their payments to MCI. That is what a manager of collections is supposed to do. This meant visits both to MCI's major ("Top Tier") clients who had billing disputes with MCI and to Tier 3 clients who just did not seem to have the money to pay for telecommunication services that they had used from MCI. Typical invoice amounts of customers in the Tier 3 group were fifty thousand dollars per month up to two million dollars per month. Whereas the majority of Top Tier customer's outstanding balances represented tens of millions of dollars in disputed amounts, it was certain that MCI would eventually get a majority of those funds once the dispute was settled. But a few million dollars with a Tier 3 customer was at risk of never being collected because of the precarious financial situation of these customers. There was also more pressure to collect these invoices because a majority of these amounts represented profits for MCI. It was not unusual for Tier 3 clients to yield profits of over one hundred percent versus the one percent or less for Top Tier customers.

My month would start by looking at an aging report of outstanding receivables and developing a plan to meet performance goals that had been set for me based on the number of days and dollar amounts that were outstanding from the day of invoicing. Most companies refer to this measurement as Days Sales Outstanding. The goal was simple: get the most cash in house in the shortest period of time.

I would go through the list of clients who owed MCI money, determine the validity of their reasons for not paying, and then set up meetings with those clients that would help MCI meet its financial goals for the month. It was exhausting.

Most business meetings are to discuss relationships, new business, and current business. But every meeting that I attended with a client was because they owed MCI money, so these meetings were intense, often with heightened tempers, tremendous pressure on both sides, and consequences that could lead to the disconnection of services, and ultimate financial ruin, for the Tier 3 customer I was visiting. It was not business as usual.

I visited a number of companies throughout 1995 as the number of Tier 3 clients and their subsequent delinquencies increased throughout the year. By the middle of 1995, MCI management knew that we had a problem with client delinquencies and the increasing amount of bad debt (uncollectable invoices) that was being experienced.

MCI's Carrier Segment had a bad debt goal of $15 million for the entire year of 1995. We had come close to that amount by the halfway point of the year, and the number of customers with delinquent balances that were most likely heading for write-off was considerably higher than we had forecast. Adding to the pressure, MCI was a target on Wall Street as a possible takeover candidate in the evolving telecommunications industry. MCI was "in play" and our financial results would be key in the amount of money a company would pay for each share. The share price became more important, so meeting our financial goals became more important as well.

As I traveled the country to negotiate with clients, I became more frustrated with my abilities to meet the financial goals that I was given. While I tried to negotiate payment terms with a number of Tier 3 customers, it seemed to me that they were simply stealing from MCI by not paying for the telecommunication services that they were using and reselling. The worst offenders were prepaid calling card companies.

These companies used MCI's network to carry the phone calls that they were selling to the public in the form of a prepaid calling card. These are the kinds of cards for sale in convenience stores as a way for those who are on a budget or have restricted access to phone service to make phone calls. Often these cards are purchased based on price alone because the networks on which they travel are very reliable. Those networks were reliable because they were operated by companies like MCI who provided the services to complete the call, while the Tier 3 carrier who was selling the card collected the cash for the card. Getting the Tier 3 carrier to pay MCI for those underlying services became a major challenge, and the task of collection fell to me to get that money into MCI.

One major player in the prepaid card arena was Caribbean Telephone and Telegraph (CT&T), based in Detroit. CT&T started on MCI's network in early 1995 with average monthly billings of fifty thousand dollars. By the later part of 1995, CT&T was billing ten million dollars per month and had fallen significantly behind on their payments to MCI.

CT&T had approximately fifty full-time employees, and they distributed prepaid calling cards in major metropolitan areas like New York, Los Angeles, and Miami. These areas offered a unique marketing approach for CT&T, as they sold prepaid cards for phone calls to specific countries. With large ethnic populations in defined areas of these cities, CT&T could print phone cards for a Chinese neighborhood just as easily as it could for a Cuban neighborhood. They sold these cards in small delis and bodegas, targeting a specific country at a discount rate that they had negotiated with MCI. It was a good business model and a very profitable account for MCI; or it would have been if CT&T had paid their bills.

As the CT&T revenue grew with MCI, so did their delinquencies on the amounts due. By July 1995, CT&T owed MCI over twenty-five million dollars in outstanding invoices. MCI needed these invoices to be paid, as it had already booked the revenue and associated profit. To replicate the amount of profit that MCI would have with a customer like CT&T, it would need billions and billions in sales from a Tier 1 customer like Sprint, WorldCom, or AT&T. That CT&T money had to make its way back to MCI.

When I visited CT&T's office in New York in July 1995 there was over twenty-five million dollars outstanding. It was a contentious meeting, where I was being monitored by MCI sales personnel so that I would not do too much to disturb such a valued customer. MCI executives were also closely monitoring my visit, as they did not want a standoff that would jeopardize the collection of those outstanding amounts. I was in a difficult position.

The visit went as well as could be expected, but the customer simply made promises about making future payments. I was also allowed to view their "collection center" that held millions of dollars in cash that had been collected from the sale of the prepaid calling cards. In a small conference room there were a number of people counting mounds of cash that had been brought in from the daily sales of calling cards. It was a good sign that there was so much money coming in, but the main question for me was why this money was not making its way to MCI.

As time went on, CT&T continued to make payments to MCI, but their payment always lagged well behind the invoice amounts due. As 1995 drew to a close, CT&T had unpaid invoices to MCI that were valued at over one hundred million dollars.

Other carrier customers were acting in similar ways but with dollar amounts that were smaller; they were in the single millions rather than the tens of millions of dollars outstanding. As I visited these Tier 3 customers I found similar promises and similar promises broken. By the end of 1995, MCI's carrier division was looking at losses that could amount to nearly two hundred million dollars.

Isolation

In late 1995 the director of billing and collections decided to leave the department to pursue other interests in MCI. In personal discussions I had with him before he left, he informed me that the pressures of the job were taking a toll on his personal life and that he wanted something with less pressure than chasing carrier customers cross country for payment. However, just as he was leaving the department, MCI executives decided to disconnect CT&T for non-payment, leaving MCI with over one hundred million dollars in unpaid invoices.

MCI was considered a prime takeover candidate in the telecommunications industry in late 1995. The industry was consolidating with merger after merger, with WorldCom leading the way, gobbling up one carrier after another. It was not a time to disclose bad financial results as the disclosure would most certainly have a negative impact on the stock price.

What to do about CT&T? Executives much higher than me or my director decided that CT&T would be offered a promissory note to sign with no collateral or personal guarantee associated with the debt. Such a move would allow MCI to move an accounts receivable of one hundred million dollars to a short-term debt, still an asset, on MCI's books. It was a move that we had used before for much smaller customer amounts to allow repayment of debt to MCI over time, usually three to five years. This one-hundred-million-dollar note dwarfed any other similar transaction that we had, but it prevented disclosure of the bad debt that the financially weak CT&T represented. It was the beginning of a series of events that led many at MCI, including me, down a dark path to financial manipulation and rationalization for actions that were clearly unethical.

One hundred million dollars of CT&T revenue was moved to the promissory note, and note payments were to begin in April 1996, one month after Arthur-Andersen would have completed its audit for the year ending 1995. There would not be a delinquent note payment from CT&T, who would essentially be out of business as a result of being disconnected, because a payment would not have been due. My director left and in came my new director.

I informed my new director of the challenges that were present in our carrier division. He had experience with these customers, so it would not take him long to get up to speed on a number of issues. During one of our meetings in late 1995, we put together a report that clearly stated that MCI's carrier division would need to have a bad debt reserve of one hundred eighty million dollars for the upcoming year 1996. We put together a great deal of supporting information on CT&T, which represented one hundred million dollars of the write-off requirement and the eighty million dollars of debt from other customers who were on a similar path of non-payment. One hundred eighty million dollars was really bad news when the typical bad debt budget had averaged fifteen million dollars in each of the previous five years. We both decided to submit this package to executives above us for consideration.

Our answer came back within a few weeks. The budget for bad debt for 1996 was going to stay at fifteen million dollars and we were to redouble our efforts to assure that there would be no further bad debts. The message was clear to me: do whatever it takes to make those numbers. Alarm bells should have gone off in my head.

I began chairing monthly meetings with accounting, business development, marketing, and planning where we discussed in detail the financial performance of the carrier division. All those in the room represented young up-and-comers in the company with an average age of approximately 30 years. The meetings would start off with me saying that I had another customer who had been disconnected for non-payment and that they owed, say, three million dollars. Rather than saying that I was going to write this off to bad debt, I would open discussions by saying, "How much can I write off this month?" The correct answer should have been, "All of it." But the answer I got was something like, "Take a million this month and then we'll see what we can do next month." What I was supposed to do with the revenue that should have been written off was not discussed further. I had to figure that out myself. I did not tell others in the group and they did not ask. We each had our own problems and challenges.

For a period of four months at the beginning of 1996 I met the financial goals that had been stated for my division, but the results that we were reporting did not match the reality of the growing number of clients that were being disconnected for non-payment. The monthly meetings with finance became more stressful and less information was being exchanged. We were all withdrawing into our own worlds to handle what we perceived to be our own problems. It became too much for me and I wanted out.

The Crime

I set up a meeting in late April 1996 with a former MCI carrier customer named "Howard Miller" (not his real name). Howard was a young man who had had success with a string of telecommunication ventures, including a dabble in 900 sex chat lines. That did not matter to me as I saw Howard as someone who knew the industry and was simply providing a service over telecommunication lines that MCI provided. He was a businessman and we got along well.

The purpose of the meeting was to let Howard know that I wanted out of MCI; I wanted a new job. I vented my frustration to him about the customers ripping off MCI and how we within MCI were hiding these bad results. He was amused with my situation and my struggles with it.

"When are you going to get it," he told me. "Everybody cheats, Walt, and you're the only one who hasn't figured out how to make money at it."

It was a telling comment that made me realize how much I had already stepped over the line and how helpless I felt to change my own direction. I still wanted to leave MCI, but Howard had another idea. He believed that he could develop a plan that would keep MCI's profitable accounts in operation, help out small telecommunications companies, and, more importantly, make us some money in the process.

"Stay right where you are, Walt, and I'll get back with you," was what he told me. And that's what I did.

Over the next few weeks I met with Howard as I continued to be frustrated by what I was doing at MCI. Finally, we had put together a plan that would clearly be one of deception and fraud. For some reason, I did not recognize the crime for what it was, but as a kind of revenge on a company and an industry that I had come to despise.

The plan was for me to approach high-risk customers and put pressure on them to pay their delinquent balances or be subjected to disconnection. This was not going to be an unusual way of conducting business. After all, I was in the business of collections and the threat of disconnection because of non-payment was a normal business practice. I targeted an MCI customer, TNI, that was based in Marietta, Georgia. TNI purchased telecommunication service from MCI and then resold it to a number of purveyors of services for sex chat, gambling, and fortune telling. TNI routinely paid their invoices late and had an outstanding accounts receivable balance of two million dollars. I demanded payment of two million dollars within two weeks or TNI was going to be disconnected.

The exchange with TNI's president was heated, and the sudden enforcement of the payment terms put them in a desperate situation. TNI would be put out of business if MCI disconnected its telecommunication services.

Within a few days of making this demand, Howard walked into the offices of TNI and posed as an investor who purchased telecommunication companies. In the eyes of TNI's president, Howard's timing could not have been better. Howard had money and TNI needed it, quickly.

Howard told the owner of TNI that he was an investor who represented other investors in Europe who were looking for telecommunication companies to purchase. TNI needed money and they opened their books for Howard and a group of accountants to quickly provide an assessment of the financial situation of the company and to determine whether or not TNI would be a suitable investment.

As the two-week deadline approached, Howard became the most powerful man in the universe to the owner of TNI. Howard had money. Howard informed TNI that they would make an excellent investment for his European investors and could help the company out with its short term cash needs with MCI.

The deal would be that Howard and his investors would lend TNI two million dollars to meet the MCI deadline in exchange for a two-hundred-and-fifty-thousand-dollar up-front fee, twenty-five percent ownership in TNI, and weekly payments of ten thousand dollars per week until the loan was either paid off or converted to an equity position. There were also promises for more money in the future from Howard and his investors. TNI thought that their prayers had been answered by this "angel" investor.

Howard informed TNI that the two million dollars was going to be paid directly to MCI from Europe and that the money would not pass through TNI. TNI would receive confirmation from MCI that their account balances had been paid with the funds transferred from the angel investor. But there was no such wire transfer or payment. In fact, the remaining part of the plan was for me to cover the debt owed to MCI by TNI and give it the appearance that in fact a debt had been paid. I did this with a series of journal voucher entries that completely wiped out the debt of TNI without ever receiving any funds on behalf of TNI.

The way that TNI's debt was hidden was that I added TNI accounts to other bad debt accounts and wrote them off to bad debt. I had figured that we were not going to collect on the amounts due anyway, so adding a few hundred thousand dollars to the debt of a customer where I had approval to write it off should not matter. In other cases I used unapplied cash from customers who had been written off years before or unapplied cash/credits from accounts where we had no idea whose cash/credits it was. The amount of unapplied cash/credit on MCI's books averaged over sixty million dollars each month, so it was not difficult to "borrow" some funds to close invoices such as those of TNI's.

I reported to my director and everyone at my monthly finance meeting that TNI was off of our watch list with a payment of two million dollars. Everyone was pleased at the news and nobody questioned the payment. No one asked me for a copy of a check or proof of a wire transfer. Had they done this, it would have revealed that in fact no payment had been received.

I sent a letter to TNI indicating that their account balance with MCI was now zero and that we had received a two-million-dollar payment. Both statements were lies. TNI began to make payments to the supposed angel investors, to bank accounts and companies set up in the Cayman Islands. There was no link to those companies and me or Howard Miller.

As the money began to flow, Howard took me on trips to Grand Cayman to visit with offshore banking professionals. Money was dispersed to other banks across the globe to further cover the tracks of the money and its origins. Over the next six months we did this same sort of transaction with seven customers and paid over six million dollars into offshore accounts. In what may seem to be a surprise to some, I was scared to death and otherwise deeply unhappy.

I used a MasterCard charge card that was linked to offshore accounts to pay for a lifestyle that was clearly beyond my means. Top restaurants, first-class vacations, and the trappings of a fast lifestyle were all part of my new-found persona. I was living two different lives, and within eight months of embarking on this crime spree, I was near a nervous breakdown. I was no longer able to function mentally, and in some cases physically, at a job in MCI that was full of pressure and the "job" of covering my tracks on a multi-million-dollar crime.

I informed Howard in late 1996 that I could no longer participate in any of these transactions. I was nervous and no longer felt in control of my life.

In January 1997 I was on business in Palm Springs, California, when I received a call from my new director who informed me that accounting had a question on a journal entry that had caught their attention. It was one of the transactions that I had done to cover my scheme with Howard, and I was being called to investigate the transaction, not as a suspect. But I could no longer hide what I had done and upon hearing the name of the account I told my boss, "I quit."

My sudden resignation was met with compassion from many within MCI who begged me to come back to work. Upon returning home to Atlanta, I went to a physician who determined that I was suffering from extreme symptoms of stress; he put me on anti-depressants and sleeping pills. Naively, I convinced myself that I could make a recovery and that the situation that I left at MCI would simply go away. But it was just getting started.

Within a few weeks the phone calls from executives at MCI who had wanted me to return to work stopped, and I began to hear rumors that an internal investigation had been launched to look at a number of transactions that were related to me and a few MCI customers. I had been caught and the pressure was building.

Within a year of my quitting MCI, I had retained a lawyer to protect me from phone calls that were now coming from MCI's internal investigation unit and to head off calls that were imminent from federal authorities who had been contacted. My lawyer received a letter that I was a target of a federal investigation, and the life that I had known was over. I was running for my life.

I moved my family (wife and two young boys) from Atlanta, Georgia, to escape press coverage that had appeared in the Wall Street Journal and the Atlanta Business Chronicle. I was not running for my own protection at that time but to protect my family, particularly my children (then ages seven and nine).

From January 1997 until August 2000 I lived a life of looking over my shoulder waiting for FBI agents to arrest me. It was continued punishment for my actions, and I searched for a way to put this experience behind me. Finally in August 2000 I asked my lawyer to negotiate my surrender and cooperation to federal authorities. I had spent hundreds of thousands of dollars on defending myself and I had not even seen the inside of a courtroom. Had I kept on going, I would have left my family with considerable debt and would have been looking at a significant prison sentence. I had to face what I had done.

I began cooperating with the FBI, IRS, and U.S. Attorney's Office in August 2000. The length of my sentence would depend on the information and accuracy of that information as it related to my crime. I had no idea how the impact of that information would affect my sentencing in federal court. As such, I did not inform anyone in my family that I had begun to cooperate with the government nor that a prison sentence was in my future. My rationale was that I could not tell my wife whether I was going to go to prison for three years or ten years. I could not bear to put someone through that anguish when I did not know the answer myself. For nearly a month I traveled to Atlanta for meetings with the FBI as I tried to determine how my cooperation would affect my sentence. By the end of August I felt comfortable that a sentence of less than five years was possible. It was time to inform my family.

Prison and Moving On

I was sentenced to forty-one months in prison and received time off my sentence for participating in a drug and alcohol abuse program within the Bureau of Prisons. My abuse of alcohol and anti-depressants had been a part of my life between 1996 and the day that I showed up at the prison. The total time that I spent in prison was over eighteen months; then I spent six months in a halfway house where I wore an ankle bracelet and had my every movement monitored.

When I finally left custody of the Bureau of Prisons in March 2003, I was financially broke, was served divorce papers from my wife of fifteen years, and had no job prospects. At the age of forty, I moved in with my parents and began to piece my life back together as best I could. I then began three years of probation, which restricts my travel and monitors my financial situation from month to month, as I make restitution payments on an amount due of six million dollars. It is quite likely that this sum—which now seems to me like a staggering amount of money—will hang over me for the rest of my life.

I began conducting speaking engagements on my experiences that same year and interviewed with a number of companies as I attempted to get back on my feet. I received no job offers and kept up with the speaking engagements to make ends meet. As of the writing of this book, I am currently self-employed and conduct lectures for federal law enforcement, business schools, professional societies, and corporations. I find this work rewarding in that I have found a way to survive while teaching others about the temptations in the business world.

I would have never pictured myself as having the ability to commit any type of white-collar crime. Like everyone else who knew me back in 1992, I truly thought of myself as a good guy, a guy who was unusual only in positive ways. Was I ambitious and eager to get ahead? Sure. Did I have a solid moral understanding? I thought so. I don't really think my moral standards have changed from 1992 until now: I thought stealing was wrong then, and I think so now. My problem was not following the moral code I have. For a brief period, that made me rich. For a long period, not yet over, it made me miserable.

The apparent, short-term rewards are utterly not worth it. I ruined my life and the lives of many close to me because I did not follow my code. The lesson I learned is a profoundly painful one. If you start to slip, stop and return to your code. The sooner you do, the happier you will be.

Before my conviction, I had no criminal record other than a speeding ticket. None of the others involved in the crime had criminal records either. All of us had college educations, were married, and had children. We all appeared to look like the guy you wanted to hire. We looked like you.

As of the writing of this book, "Howard Miller" is currently in federal prison and will be released in 2006. He will be deported to Canada upon his release, as he is a Canadian citizen, and will most likely not be eligible to return to the United States. Howard pled guilty and also cooperated with the government to avoid a trial and an almost certain lengthy prison sentence. Howard will have served four years in prison upon his release. When he entered prison, he was married and had three children. When I last talked to him, he was miserable.

It is worth stressing again that it is not enough to have a strong moral code. You have to follow that code, and you have to come back to it if you slip. Your own happiness, and probably that of many other people, depends on this.

110 *Taking the Harder Right* From Ambitious and Upwardly . . .

11 Conclusion

You have seen throughout this book how good, honest, moral, ethical people can get into trouble and the moral and ethical conflicts in our lives that can lead to disaster. If there were easy answers to these conflicts, this book and others dealing with the topic would be unnecessary. All one would have to do is go to a manual, look for the particular problem, and apply the solution. Regrettably, life is much more complicated. It has been the goal of this book to examine some of the pressures we face in our daily lives and to encourage the reader, "To take the harder right instead of the easier wrong." Taking the harder right, as we have seen, can be the hardest thing you will ever do in your life. It is the premise of this book, though, that it will serve you well despite whatever hardship is brought to bear.

The stories of Josh, Diann, and Walt are compelling for a number of reasons. They came from good families and good backgrounds. They knew right from wrong and tried to live their lives accordingly. Pressure plus rationalization in each instance led to catastrophe. Insidiousness was another ingredient. None ever saw the dire consequences of their decisions. Recall that Diann, even when she was sentenced to eighteen months in federal prison, refused to believe that it was happening to her because "good people like me don't go to prison." All three once thought that they might be participants in a seminar like *Taking the Harder Right* —in the audience, not as presenters.

Today Josh, Diann, and Walt struggle to provide for their families. Each has a job but not one that provides for benefits like health insurance, sick leave, vacation, or retirement. If they don't work, they don't get paid. Their career choices are severely limited because of the laws that proscribe convicted felons from engaging in so many occupations. Then there are the rumors and stories that go around the neighborhood and the kids' schools. And on and on. The price is enormous. For them there is no real money in sharing their message. At most it will help to defray their day-to-day living expenses. Nothing more. A presidential pardon to restore their civil rights is a far-reaching goal that lies at least ten years ahead, if ever. They have shared their stories with complete candor in the hope that there will be readers who might undergo a life-shaping or life-changing experience from it. Such life-shaping experience can result from absorbing the message of this book. A life-changing experience could be disengagement from ongoing or contemplated destructive conduct.

I hope this book or your attendance at one of our seminars has impacted you, and that you will share its message with your family, friends, and those you care about.

Oliver G. Halle

Oliver Halle spent twenty-eight years with the FBI as a special agent before retiring in August 2003. He was trained and certified by the FBI as a legal advisor and ethics instructor. His career included working organized crime in New York City and public corruption investigations for seventeen years in the Atlanta division. He graduated from Gordon Military College (now Gordon College) with a junior college degree in 1965. Halle is a graduate of Elon College, The University of North Carolina School of Law (Juris Doctor), and New York University School of Law (Master of Laws). Halle was a commissioned naval officer and served on the cruiser USS SPRINGFIELD. He was also an officer-in-charge of a Swift Boat in Vietnam and was awarded the Bronze Star with Combat V for meritorious action. Of the many professional memberships Oliver has, the most distinguished is the New York City Police Department Honor Legion. This select group appointed him for his role in the FBI/NYPD investigation and prosecution of the hierarchy of the Columbo organized crime family.

Halle has taught numerous classes to FBI agents, New York City police, Georgia police academies, and other federal agencies. He served on the Special Agents Advisory Committee for five years, an elected position that meets with the FBI Director and other senior management to discuss policy and other issues. Halle was the national chairman of this committee from 1993-1994.

Halle has had television appearances on "60 Minutes" with Ed Bradley, "The FBI: Untold Stories," and "Women in the Mafia," all in connection with his work on the Columbo case.

He was also profiled in the book, *Mob Girl* (Simon & Schuster, 1992) by Pulitzer-Prize-winning author Theresa Carpenter.

Halle is the president of Oliver G. Halle & Associates, Inc., www.CorporateScaredStraight.com. The company office address is 2100 Roswell Road N.E., Suite 200 C-PMB 521, Marietta, GA 30062. Telephone: 770/321-2778.

INDEX

Numerals

1996 Olympic Games 50
53668-019 *See* Cattani, Diann
"60 Minutes"—television show 113

A

abortion 9
accountability 76
accountants 76, 77, 103
accounting department 22
Alfieri, Conte Vittorio 71
anticorruption 4
AT&T 92, 93, 94, 98
Atlanta 29, 49, 50, 52, 53, 64, 73, 74, 82, 87, 91, 106, 107
Atlanta Braves 74
Atlanta Business Chronicle 107
attorney 3, 18, 20, 29, 30, 31, 50, 58, 66, 77
Auschwitz: A New History 12
Australia 40

B

BellSouth 58
"Best, Michael" 52, 53
Bible 9
billable hours 18
Blatt, Toivi 12
Blockbuster 74, 75, 77
boss 10, 18, 24, 30, 56, 66, 106
bribe 11, 16, 17, 30, 56, 60, 61
Brigham Young University 5, 73, 74
Brown University ix

Buck, Esther 40, 41
Buckhead (section of Atlanta, Georgia) 51
Buckner, Ed and Diane x, xi
Bush, President George and Barbara 74

C

cadet prayer v, 5
Canada 109
Cardwell, Dale 87
Caribou Coffee 55, 56, 57
Carpenter, Theresa 114
Cather, Willa 2
Catholic 9
Cattani, Diann iii, x, xi,, 5, 37, 47, 71, 83, 111
Cayman Islands 105
"Center" County, Georgia 50, 51, 53, 60
Certified Fraud Examiner 77
Certified Public Accountant 50, 77
character 15, 27, 35, 37, 40, 51, 62
cheating in school 20
Christian 9, 50, 72
Christian Coalition 50
Christmas 21, 53, 68, 76
church 9, 11, 12, 23, 81
Clinton administration 20
Club Fed 84
Columbo organized crime family 113
communion 9
Constitution, U.S. 9
corruption 25, 26, 49, 64, 66
CT&T 97, 98, 99, 100
culture of honesty 88
culture of integrity 88

D

Donne, John   85
duty   9, 40, 47

E

Einstein's Coffee House   64
Elon College   113
eternal punishment   36
ethical compass   1, 15, 25, 47, 53, 88
ethical imperatives   8
ethical principles   15, 7, 13
ethical quandaries   9
ethics   11, 12, 13, 4, 7, 8, 9, 12, 18, 25, 51
evil   71, 72, 92

F

fail with honor   10, 11
FBI   ix, xi, 1, 2, 3, 4, 10, 29, 30, 31, 40, 55, 56, 60, 64, 66, 67, 107, 113
"The FBI: Untold Stories"—television show   113
federal prison   5, 20, 49, 68, 82, 92, 109, 111
felon   17, 23, 33, 86
foundations of morality   12
fraud   1, 4, 10, 11, 20, 22, 23, 24, 77, 102
fraud triangle   77
fraudulent expense accounts   21
Ft. Worth, Texas   49

G

gambling   93, 103
Gartland, Pat   50
GEC Avionics, Inc.   91
Germany   9, 41

Gingrich, Newt (former Speaker, U.S. House)   88
girlfriend   21, 62, 63, 64
God   30, 36
Goger, Superior Court Judge John   66
good people   1, 15
Goodyear Aerospace   91
Gordon College (formerly Gordon Military College)   113
"Grange, George"   54, 55, 56, 57, 58, 60, 61, 63, 64, 65
Groundhog Day   68

H

Halle, Caitlyn   x
Halle, Knut and Ruth   vii
Halle, Mollie   x
Halle, Oliver G.   56, 64, 66, 113
Halle, Tyler   x
Halle, Victoria   x
Hamm, Commander Warren C.   ix
Hawaii   74
"Higginworth, Michael"   65, 66, 67
Hubbell, Webster   20

I

Idaho   72
income taxes   60, 64, 66
informants   10
"inmate Kenyon"   69
insidious   22, 23, 80
internal affairs   26
Internal Revenue Service (IRS)   30, 107

J

Jefferson, Thomas   88
Jewish   9, 41, 42

K

Kennedy, U.S. Senator Ted   21
Kenyon, Eliza   68
Kenyon, Josh   iii, x, xi, 5, 49, 111
Kenyon, Morgan   68
Kenyon, Shelly   57, 58, 62, 65
Kerry, U.S. Senator John   9
kickback(s)   16, 17
Korean War   46

L

Las Vegas   61, 62
leadership and ethics   13
leadership skills   45
life-changing versus life-shaping events or experiences   15, 39, 82, 112
Lutheran   42

M

Mare Island, California   45
marriage   5, 17, 21, 60, 62, 63, 80
Mayr, Ernst   8
McCain, U.S. Senator John   47
MCI Telecommunications   91, 92, 93, 94, 95, 96, 97, 98, 99, 100, 102, 103, 104, 105, 106
mentor   18, 20, 53, 86
Mercer University   5, 91
Military Code of Conduct   46
"Miller, Howard"   102, 105, 109
Mob Girl   114
Morris, Bruce   66

N

Navy, U.S.   13, 40, 46
Nazi   12, 41, 42
NCAA   73

New York   2, 3, 10, 27, 41, 97, 98, 113
New York University   113

O

Oliver G. Halle & Associates, Inc.   114
"Oprah"—televison show. *See* Winfrey, Oprah.
organized crime   3, 10, 113

P

Pavlo, Walt   iii, x, 91, 111
PCF 692   39
Pepperdine University   5, 49
"perfect" mom   78
police officer   25, 35, 36
polygraph   3, 4
pornography   93
POW   45, 46
presidential pardon   112
prohibited source   22
Protestant   41
Providence, Rhode Island   49
public corruption   55

R

rationalization   19, 77
Rees, Lawrence   12
religious faith   35
Republican   50, 51
Romeo Mike   15, 2, 29, 30, 31, 32, 49
Rose law firm   20

S

school teacher 40
Schuerholz, John (General Mgr., Atlanta Braves) 74
Schweitzer, Albert 72
Securities and Exchange Commission 2, 3
sibling rivalry 72
Socrates 83
Sophocles 10
Southeastern Legal Foundation 50
Southern Methodist University 5, 49
Special Agents Advisory Committee 113
Sprint 92, 93, 94, 98
"Stanley, Matthew" 50, 51, 52, 56, 60, 66
Star-Spangled Banner 46
Steamhouse Lounge 64
Story, Federal Judge Richard 66
Swift Boat 39, 45, 113

T

tax evasion 61
Ten Commandments 8
Thanksgiving 82
Third Reich 41
Thoreau, Henry David 2
TNI 103, 104, 105
true north 15
Tucker, FBI Agent Joe 65, 67
Turkey 81, 82
turnstile justice 25

U

U.S. Attorney 66, 67, 107
United States Military Academy *See* West Point
University of North Carolina 113
USS SPRINGFIELD ix, 113
Utah 72, 73, 76, 81

V

Vietnam 39, 40, 47, 113
volleyball 72, 73, 75

W

Wachtler, Sol 27
Wall Street Journal 107
Wayman, Kim iv, ix
West Point v, 5-6
Whidbey Island, Washington 45
white collar crime 1
White House 74
Winfrey, Oprah (and "Oprah"— television show) 80
"Women in the Mafia"—television show 113
WorldCom 91, 92, 93, 94, 98, 99

Z

Zech, Captain Lando ix